THE GIFT OF ADMINISTRATION
CALLED TO ORGANISE. ANOINTED TO SERVE.

By Frances Grace

© 2025 Frances Grace Consulting Limited

All rights reserved. No part of this book may be reproduced, stored in a retrieval system, or transmitted in any form or by any means, electronic, mechanical, photocopying, recording, or otherwise, without the prior written permission of the publisher.

ISBN: 978-1-8383824-3-8

Publisher: Frances Grace Consulting Limited

Email: hello@francesgraceconsulting.com

Dedication

To every unsung administrator building God's house behind the scenes — thank you. Your labour is not in vain. Heaven sees what no one else may notice. Keep building. Keep leading. Keep running your race.

With love and honour,

Frances Grace

Acknowledgements

This book would not have been possible without the love, encouragement, and support of many people who have stood with me on this journey.

To God — my ultimate source of wisdom, creativity, and peace. You placed this burden in my heart and sustained me through every word. May this offering glorify You and serve Your Church.

To my husband, Dee — thank you for your unwavering belief in me. Your spiritual strength, patience, and love are a constant anchor. You have covered our family with prayer, encouraged me to press on, and reminded me why this message matters.

To Daniella and Adele — my daughters, my joy. You inspire me daily to lead with purpose, integrity, and grace. Your support means more than words can express.

To my mum, Lovett Yemi — your resilience and faith have shaped the woman I am today. Thank you for teaching me to persevere, to give generously, and to always walk in the light of God's Word. Thank you, too, for the countless hours you have spent praying for me — covering my life, my calling, and my family with intercession. Your prayers have been a shield, a breakthrough, and a blessing. I am walking in answered prayers today because of you.

To every church leader and administrator who has poured into my life or welcomed my gift — thank you. Your example and encouragement have helped refine my calling. This book is for you.

CALLED TO ORGANISE. ANOINTED TO SERVE.

To my mentors and ministry peers — thank you for your wisdom, feedback, and prayers. Your voices strengthened mine when I needed it most.

To the readers — thank you for investing your time in this book. I pray you feel seen, equipped, and empowered to walk boldly in your administrative calling.

About the Author

Frances Grace is a worship leader, church administrator, business safety consultant, and writer with over 25 years of experience serving in ministry.

Throughout her journey, she has worked closely with churches across various denominations, leading worship teams and strengthening church operations through her administrative gifting.

Frances is passionate about empowering leaders to embrace the often-overlooked gift of administration and see it as a vital part of Kingdom work.

Alongside her husband—who serves in prayer ministry—they are both elders in their local church, committed to mentoring others and building up the body of Christ.

She is also a devoted mother to two young adult daughters and continues to encourage families to walk faithfully in their God-given calling.

Table of Contents

Dedication iii
Acknowledgements iv
About the Author. vi
1: Introduction – Unveiling the Gift of Administration .1
2: The Biblical Foundation of Administration 7
3: The Fivefold Ministry and Spiritual Gifts 14
4: Misconceptions About the Gift of Administration. 21
5: The Administrator vs. The Visionary 27
6: Church Administration in the 21st Century 35
7: The Remote Church – Administration in a Digital Age 43
8: The Administrator's Role in Church Growth. 51
9: Challenges Administrators Face in the Church 59
10: Taming the Wild Horse – Nurturing the Gift of Administration. 68
11: The Gift of Administration in the Secular Workplace 75
12: Case Studies and Lessons from Real Church Administrators 83
13: Navigating Leadership Conflicts 90
14: Building Effective Teams with the
    Right Leadership Structures 98
15: Beyond the Four Walls – Interest Groups
    and Community Impact 106
16: A Call to Action – The Future of Church Administration. 115
17: Preparing the Ground – Positioning the Gift for Greater Impact 122
18: Developing Administrative Leaders 127

19:	The Administrator's Spiritual Life	132
20:	Leading Through Transition and Crisis	137
21:	Leaving a Legacy	142
22:	Reframing Excellence – Doing Ministry Well	146
23:	Creating a Culture of Honour in Administration	149
24:	Spiritual Discernment in Administrative Decision-Making	153
25:	Ministering to Volunteers and Ministry Teams	158
26:	Reimagining Church Operations for Future Growth	164
27:	The Role of the Administrator in Church Planting	170
28:	How to Build a Healthy Administrative Team	175
29:	Administrative Wisdom for Multicultural Churches	181
30:	Digital Tools and Systems for Modern Church Administration	187
31:	Measuring Impact and Evaluating Ministry Health	194
32:	The Administrator as a Bridge Builder	201
33:	The Calling and Commissioning of the Administrator	207

Introduction – Unveiling the Gift of Administration

Administration is one of the most vital yet consistently undervalued gifts in the body of Christ. Often hidden in the shadows of what are perceived to be more visible or charismatic ministries, administration is frequently misunderstood. In many churches, it is mistakenly equated with clerical support — as though taking minutes, filing papers, and scheduling meetings is the sum total of what administrators do. But this is a limited and ultimately misleading view. Scripture reveals a far richer and more significant picture. The gift of administration is not merely functional; it is deeply spiritual. It is a Spirit-empowered calling designed to bring divine order, clarity, strategy, and structure to the vision God gives His people.

In 1 Corinthians 12:28, the Apostle Paul outlines the variety of gifts God has placed within the church: "And God has appointed in the church first apostles, second prophets, third teachers, then miracles, then gifts of healing, helping, administrating, and various kinds of tongues." The word translated here as "administration" or "guidance" comes from the Greek term *kybernesis* — a nautical word referring to the steering of a ship. This is the image God gives us: not of someone shuffling paperwork in the background, but of a helmsman, someone who steers the vessel through turbulent waters, guiding it safely toward its destination.

This paints administration not as a passive role, but as an active, intentional, and courageous one. The administrator, in this light, is someone who takes the prophetic word and gives it legs; someone who receives a God-given vision and helps build the pathways for that vision to be fulfilled. Far from being a secondary player, the administrator is a strategic leader, quietly but decisively keeping the mission on course.

Having served for over two decades in ministry, both as a worship leader and as a church administrator, I have experienced the breadth and depth of this gift. I have witnessed how it brings balance, flow, and sustainability to ministries. I have also felt the weight of it — the tension between being essential and yet invisible. There have been countless times when administrators have poured hours of work into an event, a service, or a new system, only to have their efforts go unnoticed. The applause often goes to those on stage, while those behind the scenes fade into the background. Yet the impact of their work is undeniable.

Without administration, churches flounder. Events are disorganised, communication breaks down, volunteers become overworked and undervalued, and resources are often wasted. More dangerously, the lack of structure can cause vision to be lost altogether. The truth is sobering: many churches do not fail because they lack passion, powerful preaching, or persistent prayer — they fail because they lack structure. Vision alone is not enough. Without a framework to carry it, the vision collapses under its own weight.

The gift of administration is the skeletal system of the church. Just as the body needs bones to give it form and enable movement, the church needs administration to provide order and direction. Without bones, the body cannot stand. Without administration, the church struggles to move forward.

This book was born out of a deep desire to see this gift recognised, honoured, and developed across the global church. Too many administrators serve in isolation, undervalued and overworked. Too many pastors try to carry the burden of leadership without the necessary administrative support. And too many churches misunderstand the divine significance of this gift. My prayer is that this book will serve as both a mirror and a map — a mirror that reflects the beauty of what God has placed in administrators, and a map that guides us toward greater effectiveness and understanding.

Whether you are a full-time church administrator, a volunteer leading a small ministry team, a pastor doing it all with minimal support, or someone who senses a call to bring structure to vision, this book is for you. You might be the person who builds spreadsheets, writes policies, coordinates calendars, or devises strategic plans — and you may have never considered your work as "spiritual." But I want you to know: it is.

In this opening chapter, we will explore a foundational understanding of the gift of administration. We will clarify what it is, debunk myths about what it is not, and underscore why it is absolutely essential to the health, growth, and longevity of the church. We will begin a journey of reimagining administration — not as a list of tasks to be completed, but as a divine calling to be embraced.

What is the Gift of Administration?

The gift of administration is the Spirit-empowered ability to organise people, manage resources, and direct activities toward the fulfilment of a God-given mission. It marries the practical with the spiritual. It requires systems thinking, attention to detail, and strategic foresight — but it also demands discernment, wisdom, and a heart of servant leadership.

Administrators are the bridge between inspiration and implementation. Where visionaries dream of what could be, administrators ask, "How can we get there?" They are the ones who chart the course, assign responsibilities, and ensure that the vision does not die in the realm of good intentions. Their presence ensures that ministry efforts are sustainable, scalable, and effective.

Some administrators are highly detail-oriented, capable of building precise systems that ensure smooth operations. Others are more visionary, excelling in organisational strategy and tea development. Many have a combination of both. What they all have in common is a God-given instinct to bring clarity where there is confusion and direction where there is drift. They have an innate desire to see things work well — not for their own glory, but so that the Kingdom of God can flourish in excellence and integrity.

This is not a lesser gift. It is not a side role. It is a calling — a leadership mantle. It demands emotional intelligence, spiritual maturity, and resilience. The best administrators do not simply keep things tidy; they steward vision, people, and resources with intentionality and care.

Why Administration is a Spiritual Gift

One of the most damaging misconceptions in the church today is that administration is somehow secular — a necessary evil rather than a God-given grace. But this couldn't be further from the truth. Scripture affirms administration as a spiritual gift, explicitly mentioned in Paul's list of charismata in 1 Corinthians 12. It is a gift given by the Holy Spirit for the building up of the body of Christ.

Consider Exodus 18, where Jethro advises Moses to appoint capable men to help judge the people. This was not just wise counsel — it was a divine blueprint for delegation and shared responsibility. Moses was overwhelmed and unable to lead the people effectively. Jethro's administrative insight preserved both the leader and the community. This is administration in action: structure introduced to prevent burnout, promote clarity, and maintain order.

In Acts 6, we see the early church facing a logistical crisis. The apostles, overwhelmed by the daily distribution of food, wisely appointed deacons to oversee the task so they could focus on prayer and teaching. This administrative decision was not only practical — it was spiritual. It allowed the church to grow without compromising its mission. Every major move of God recorded in the Bible involved clear roles, responsibilities, and a structure to support it. God is not a God of chaos, but of order.

From the creation account in Genesis, to the meticulous instructions for building the tabernacle, to the way Jesus organised His disciples and sent them out two by two — administration is woven into the fabric of God's dealings with humanity.

You Are Not Alone

If you have ever felt overlooked, invisible, or unimportant in your role as an administrator, I want you to hear this clearly: you are not alone. Your work matters. It matters to the people you serve, to the leaders you support, and most importantly, it matters to God.

You are not just pushing paper — you are preserving vision. You are not simply coordinating events — you are building platforms where others can encounter God. Your systems make space for ministry to flourish. Your plans enable pastors to preach with focus. Your structure enables volunteers to serve with joy. Your presence often makes the difference between chaos and peace.

One of the enemy's most subtle strategies is to cause administrators to feel isolated — to believe that their work is insignificant, or that they are "less spiritual" than others. But nothing could be further from the truth. You are walking in a spiritual calling. You are a critical part of the body. And your presence at the wheel of the ship is keeping it steady.

THE GIFT OF ADMINISTRATION

As we journey through the rest of this book, I pray that you will rediscover the value and beauty of the gift of administration. May your heart be lifted, your spirit refreshed, and your hands equipped for the good work ahead.

You are not an afterthought. You are a helmsman. And the church needs you at the wheel.

The Biblical Foundation of Administration

The gift of administration is not a modern innovation or the by-product of Western church culture. It is not the result of corporate strategy entering the sacred. Instead, it is deeply rooted in the story of God and the formation of His people. From Genesis to Revelation, Scripture is full of examples that reveal God's value for order, stewardship, and wise planning. The Bible does not separate the spiritual from the strategic — in fact, it often marries the two. Administration is not a distraction from the work of God; it is part of how God works.

Throughout the biblical narrative, we are introduced to men and women whose leadership was marked by clear organisation, delegation, and systems thinking. We see that God honours planning, values order, and expects His people to steward vision with wisdom. In today's church, where the pressure for spiritual outcomes is high, many still forget that divine order is a foundational principle of growth. Passion is powerful, but without administration, passion can quickly turn into chaos.

This chapter explores the biblical case for administration, establishing it as not only practical but deeply spiritual. It is not a gift given as an afterthought — it reflects the very nature of God.

God's Nature as Administrator

We begin with the ultimate model of administration: God Himself.

Genesis 1 opens not with chaos, but with creation. The Spirit of God hovers over the formless void, and God begins to bring structure out of the shapeless. His actions are purposeful and systematic. He does not create man before creating land, nor does He form the sea before setting boundaries. Instead, God follows a divinely intentional sequence. He separates light from darkness, sky from sea, land from water — and once the environment is ordered, He fills it with life.

This pattern — first forming, then filling — reveals God's administrative nature. He establishes a framework before populating it, a rhythm before function. He introduces the cycle of day and night, the movement of the seasons, and the balance of ecosystems. All of creation bears witness to divine order. The universe is not accidental; it is structured, precise, and sustained by systems — natural and spiritual.

This image of God as both Creator and Administrator is echoed throughout the Old Testament. In Exodus 25–31, God gives Moses detailed instructions for the tabernacle — so precise they read like an architectural blueprint. Every material, measurement, and design element is specified. God not only wants to be worshipped in spirit and in truth but also within a sacred structure designed to reflect His holiness.

These passages challenge the notion that spirituality must be spontaneous and unstructured to be authentic. God, who is omniscient and all-powerful, still chooses to work through processes. His ways are ordered. His plans are intentional. And His methods involve stewardship.

Nehemiah: The Strategic Rebuilder

Nehemiah stands out as one of the Bible's most remarkable administrative leaders. When he heard of the broken walls of Jerusalem, his first response was prayer — not panic. He mourned, fasted, and interceded. But he didn't stop there. His prayer led to planning. His burden led to strategy.

Nehemiah sought permission from King Artaxerxes, secured the necessary resources, and organised the reconstruction effort with astonishing wisdom. He didn't act alone. He inspected the damage, mobilised teams, assigned responsibilities, and established systems for protection and progress. Each family worked on a different section of the wall. Leaders were placed at vulnerable points. Guards were stationed with trumpets to signal trouble.

In just 52 days, Jerusalem's walls were rebuilt. Not only because of divine favour — although that was certainly present — but because of strategic leadership and structured action. Nehemiah's story is not merely about rebuilding walls; it's about rebuilding a people with order, identity, and resilience.

Nehemiah teaches us that administrative leadership is more than logistics. It is vision translated into action. His life shows us that planning and prayer are not opposites — they are partners. Spirit-led administration involves deep communion with God and practical wisdom to lead people well.

Moses and Jethro: The Call to Delegate

In Exodus 18, we encounter one of the most pivotal administrative moments in Scripture. Moses, trying to lead the entire nation of Israel on his own, finds himself exhausted and overwhelmed. From morning until evening, he judges every dispute among the people — a heavy and unsustainable load.

His father-in-law, Jethro, observes this and offers timeless wisdom: "What you are doing is not good. You and these people who come to you will only wear yourselves out. The work is too heavy for you; you cannot handle it alone" (Exodus 18:17–18).

Jethro's solution? Delegation. He encourages Moses to appoint capable, trustworthy leaders over groups of thousands, hundreds, fifties, and tens. This not only relieves Moses but empowers others to serve. It decentralises power and multiplies effectiveness.

This principle is foundational to biblical administration. It acknowledges human limitations and affirms shared leadership. It demonstrates that God never intended for one person to carry the weight of vision alone. Wise administration builds teams, develops leaders, and releases capacity.

Jesus: Master of Organisation

While Jesus is often celebrated for His compassion, power, and divine authority, His organisational capacity is sometimes overlooked. Yet the Gospels reveal a Messiah who was deeply strategic and purposeful in the way He structured His ministry.

He chose twelve disciples — not by accident, but as a symbol of the twelve tribes of Israel, reflecting continuity and intentionality. He trained them, gave them clear instructions, and often sent them out in pairs for accountability and mutual support (Mark 6:7).

In the feeding of the 5,000 (Mark 6:39–40), Jesus doesn't distribute the food chaotically. He commands the crowd to sit down in groups on the green grass, organising them into hundreds and fifties. This moment reveals His appreciation for order, even in the midst of miracles.

Even His approach to timing was precise. Jesus often said, "My time has not yet come," reflecting a divine calendar to which He submitted. His death and resurrection occurred during Passover — not by coincidence, but in fulfilment of God's redemptive timetable.

Jesus' ministry teaches us that structure does not quench the Spirit — it makes room for the Spirit to move freely and fruitfully.

The Early Church: Organised for Growth

The Book of Acts describes the birth and explosive growth of the early church. But growth brought challenges. In Acts 6, the Greek-speaking widows were being overlooked in the daily distribution of food. The apostles recognised the problem and responded with administrative wisdom. They called for the appointment of seven trustworthy, Spirit-filled men to oversee the task.

They didn't dismiss the issue. They didn't spiritualise it away. They delegated it.

This pivotal moment shows us that the early church was willing to create new structures in response to real needs. Their solution wasn't just reactive — it was proactive. By empowering others to serve in practical roles, the apostles were free to focus on teaching and prayer.

The result? "The word of God spread; the number of disciples in Jerusalem increased rapidly" (Acts 6:7). Growth followed structure. Administration supported spiritual breakthrough.

Biblical Terms and Language

Scripture doesn't just demonstrate administrative principles — it uses specific words to describe them:

Kybernesis (1 Corinthians 12:28) – This Greek word is translated as "guidance" or "administration." It literally refers to steering, governing, or piloting a ship. It suggests direction, oversight, and control. Those with this gift are not passengers — they are helmsmen.

Oikonomia (Ephesians 1:10, 1 Corinthians 9:17) – Often translated as "stewardship" or "administration," this word refers to the management of a household or the dispensation of responsibilities. It reflects the trust given to a servant to manage the affairs of a household on behalf of the master.

These words reflect divine trust, responsibility, and structure. They confirm that administration is not incidental — it is essential to the work of the Kingdom.

Administration is Ministry

Today, many churches unintentionally separate ministry into two categories: spiritual and practical. Preaching, prayer, and worship are seen as "ministry," while planning, budgeting, and scheduling are seen as "support." But this division is not biblical.

Ministry happens in the pulpit and in the planning room. It happens during a sermon and in the setup. An administrator who coordinates volunteers for a baptism service is not less spiritual than the person performing the baptism. Both are necessary. Both are ministry.

When churches undervalue administration, they compromise their ability to steward revival, care for people, and sustain growth. Emotion may ignite momentum, but administration carries it forward.

The call to administration is not a call to paperwork. It is a call to stewardship. It is a call to build structures that protect people, maximise impact, and honour God. It is a call to organise environments where the Spirit can move freely — not in chaos, but in community, with clarity and direction.

You Are Walking in Biblical Footsteps

As we continue this journey, I want to remind you: administration is not a side task. It is not an afterthought. It is God's idea — woven into the very fabric of Scripture. It is as essential as preaching, as spiritual as worship, and as powerful as prayer.

When you lead teams, manage budgets, coordinate people, plan events, or design systems, you are doing more than keeping the church running — you are helping the church thrive.

You walk in the footsteps of Nehemiah, who rebuilt a city. Of Jethro, who gave a leader wisdom. Of Jesus, who organised a movement that changed the world. You stand in the same Spirit as the early church, who understood that growth without structure is unsustainable.

You are not just helping the vision — you are fulfilling it.

The Fivefold Ministry and Spiritual Gifts

The church is not a building or a brand — it is a living, breathing body. Each part has a role to play, each member carries a divine deposit, and each gift matters. One of the clearest explanations of this design is found in Ephesians 4:11–12, where Paul writes, "So Christ himself gave the apostles, the prophets, the evangelists, the pastors and teachers, to equip his people for works of service, so that the body of Christ may be built up."

This passage, often referred to as the foundation of the "fivefold ministry," outlines five key leadership gifts given by Jesus to the church. These gifts are not merely titles; they are functions. They are tools given by Christ for the purpose of building, equipping, and maturing His people.

While these gifts are often emphasised in teachings on church leadership, there is another gift that is often overlooked — the gift of administration. Without it, the fivefold ministry struggles to operate at its full potential. The apostle may cast vision, but without implementation, the vision fades. The pastor may care deeply for the flock, but without a structure for follow-up and support, people fall through the cracks. The evangelist may draw in crowds, but without processes for connection and discipleship, they do not stay.

This chapter explores the vital harmony between the fivefold ministry and the gift of administration. Far from being a silent servant in the shadows, the administrator is a key player in the strategic advancement of the Kingdom. When working together, these gifts form a leadership ecosystem that is both Spirit-led and structurally sound.

The Fivefold Ministry Explained

Let's begin by briefly outlining the functions of the fivefold gifts. Each one carries a distinct grace and role within the church:

Apostles – These are the visionaries, pioneers, and spiritual architects. Apostles are often called to plant churches, break new ground, and establish foundations where none previously existed. They are builders, motivated by mission and long-term transformation.

Prophets – These individuals are deeply attuned to the heart and mind of God. They hear, discern, and declare God's will, often bringing correction, clarity, or encouragement. Prophets help keep the church aligned with God's purpose and timing.

Evangelists – Evangelists are the passionate communicators of the Gospel. They are gifted at connecting with unbelievers, igniting revival, and stirring the church to reach the lost. Their ministry reminds the church to look outward and multiply.

Pastors – Also called shepherds, pastors nurture and care for the flock. They build community, protect the vulnerable, and walk closely with people through life's highs and lows. Pastors provide emotional and spiritual covering.

Teachers – Teachers are communicators of truth who bring depth and clarity to the Word of God. They help believers grow in knowledge and understanding, building strong doctrinal foundations.

These roles are spiritual and strategic. Each has its own area of focus and responsibility, yet they are meant to function interdependently — not in isolation. But what keeps them coordinated, supported, and aligned? This is where the gift of administration enters the conversation.

The Missing Link: Administrators

Imagine a church led by a dynamic apostle, a prophetic intercessor, a zealous evangelist, a compassionate pastor, and a gifted teacher — but without anyone to coordinate their schedules, manage logistics, facilitate communication, or track discipleship. Despite all the gifting, the church would likely be a place of confusion, burnout, and disorganisation. Vision would remain unrealised, and ministry leaders would feel overstretched.

This is the void that administrators are born to fill. They are the ones who:

- Coordinate calendars and facilitate communication between departments.
- Build systems for pastoral care, follow-up, and discipleship.
- Track engagement and participation in small groups, ministries, and events.
- Create budgets, manage finances, and ensure resources are used wisely.
- Develop workflows for church-wide operations, from event planning to new member integration.
- Ensure each ministry aligns with the overarching vision of the church.

Administrators bring cohesion to the various moving parts of ministry. They don't replace the fivefold — they empower them. They are not competitors; they are collaborators. Their strength lies in the ability to support, organise, and sustain ministry work so that it is not just inspired, but impactful.

Biblical Harmony Between Gifts

Scripture reveals the value of administrative gifting operating alongside spiritual leadership. In Acts 6, the apostles were leading a rapidly growing church. The distribution of food to widows had become an issue, causing tension between groups. Rather than neglect the spiritual work of prayer and the Word, the apostles appointed seven qualified individuals to oversee this task.

This wasn't just delegation — it was administration. It was a strategic move that recognised that spiritual leadership must be supported by structure. The apostles continued in their calling, and the new administrators stepped in to care for practical needs. The result? "The word of God spread. The number of disciples in Jerusalem increased rapidly" (Acts 6:7).

In 1 Corinthians 12, Paul lists "administration" alongside other spiritual gifts. It is not less sacred. It is not secondary. It is part of the divine design for the church.

When these gifts function together — apostles dreaming, pastors shepherding, teachers teaching, and administrators organising — the church becomes a well-oiled machine, not just surviving, but thriving.

Working Together: A Ministry Profile

To visualise how the fivefold ministry and administration work in harmony, let's imagine the launch of a new church:

- The apostle casts a bold vision for planting a new congregation in an unreached area.

- The prophet intercedes, discerns spiritual resistance, and offers timely words that confirm and guide the vision.
- The evangelist spreads the word, gathers interest, and shares the Gospel with the community.
- The pastor begins nurturing early attendees, offering support, building relationships, and guiding people into deeper connection.
- The teacher creates curriculum for foundational Bible classes, helping new believers understand the Word of God.

But without the administrator:

> Who organises the venue?
>
> Who coordinates outreach events and builds registration systems?
>
> Who tracks volunteer availability and manages scheduling?
>
> Who ensures budgets are in place and timelines are followed?
>
> Who documents the process and keeps leadership meetings productive?

The administrator is the one who connects all the moving pieces. Their contribution is not glamorous, but it is essential. With them, a God-inspired vision becomes a real-world reality.

Equipping the Saints

Ephesians 4:12 tells us that the fivefold gifts exist "to equip his people for works of service." The administrator, although not always listed among the five, plays a critical role in this equipping process.

Administrators empower others to serve by:

> Creating role descriptions and ministry manuals.
>
> Developing volunteer onboarding systems and training schedules.

Building communication tools and feedback loops.

Removing logistical barriers that prevent people from stepping into ministry.

Ensuring safety, accountability, and order in every ministry area.

When churches honour and invest in administration, they cultivate environments where more people can serve, and serve well. Instead of being hindered by confusion or mismanagement, ministry flows smoothly. Instead of leaders wearing multiple hats, responsibilities are shared. Instead of burnout, there is balance.

Administration doesn't suffocate the Spirit — it stewards it. When the gift is present, the church is prepared not only for growth but for longevity.

When the Gift is Missing

Sadly, many churches have yet to fully recognise or release the gift of administration. As a result, they experience chronic dysfunction — not because of a lack of anointing, but because of a lack of structure.

Signs that the gift of administration is missing in a ministry include:

Ministry leaders are constantly overwhelmed and doing tasks outside their calling.

Important details fall through the cracks, leading to avoidable mistakes.

Follow-up with visitors or new believers is inconsistent or non-existent.

Communication between departments is poor, creating silos.

Events feel rushed or disorganised due to lack of planning.

Finances are mismanaged or unclear.

Volunteers are frustrated due to lack of direction or preparation.

These issues are not always the result of a lack of faith, prayer, or passion. Often, they are administrative gaps — and God has already given the solution. He has placed within the body people with a unique gift to fill this space: administrators.

Final Thoughts

The fivefold ministry and the gift of administration are not in competition. They were never meant to operate in isolation. God designed them to work together in harmony.

Some carry vision, others carry it out. Some proclaim the Word; others prepare the room. Together, they reflect the fullness of Christ's ministry to the church.

If you are an administrator, do not downplay your calling. You are not "just the organiser." You are part of God's leadership framework. Your spreadsheets, timelines, checklists, and workflows are not distractions — they are divine tools that help sustain revival, support the saints, and steward Kingdom resources.

And if you are a fivefold minister, recognise the gift of administration around you. Honour it. Empower it. Partner with it. When you do, your ministry will flourish — not only in inspiration, but in implementation.

Together, we build the church — not in chaos, but with purpose. Not with burnout, but with balance. And as each part does its work, the whole body grows, strengthened in love and unified in grace.

Misconceptions About the Gift of Administration

Despite its vital role in the church and its explicit mention in Scripture, the gift of administration remains one of the most misunderstood and undervalued spiritual gifts. The very word administration can conjure images of desks, filing cabinets, and repetitive office tasks — a far cry from the dynamic, Spirit-led calling that it truly is.

As a result, countless individuals who carry this gift feel dismissed, overlooked, or boxed into roles that do not reflect the fullness of their calling. Worse still, churches often suffer from underdeveloped systems, disorganised ministries, and leadership fatigue simply because they have misunderstood — or even ignored — the gift of administration.

In this chapter, we will confront and dismantle some of the most common myths that have distorted our understanding of this gift. By debunking these misconceptions, we will pave the way for a renewed appreciation of administration as a powerful, spiritual, and strategic gift that strengthens the Church and glorifies God.

Myth 1: Administrators Are Just Secretaries

One of the most persistent stereotypes is that administrators are essentially secretaries — that their role is limited to office duties such as answering phones, taking notes, filing paperwork, and managing emails. While some administrative tasks overlap with these responsibilities, the spiritual gift of administration extends far beyond clerical work.

Secretaries provide support, but administrators provide structure. Secretaries record decisions, but administrators often help shape them. The administrator's role involves leadership, discernment, problem solving, strategic thinking, and people management. They are the glue that holds vision together, the navigators who chart the course from concept to completion.

In Scripture, we see that godly administrators do not merely "assist" — they lead. Consider Nehemiah: he wasn't the scribe or assistant to the vision; he was the leader who brought a national restoration to life. He planned, appointed, organised, and resolved. What he accomplished in 52 days would have been impossible without the authority, wisdom, and gifting of a true administrator.

The idea that administration is a lower-tier function does not come from the Bible — it comes from cultural assumptions. And those assumptions must be challenged.

Myth 2: Administration Isn't a Spiritual Gift

Perhaps the most damaging misconception is that administration is not a spiritual gift at all. Many Christians see it as a natural talent or professional skill — something you either learn in the workplace or inherit as a personality trait. As a result, they see administration as useful but not spiritual.

But Scripture tells us otherwise.

In 1 Corinthians 12:28, administration (often translated as "guidance" or "governing") is listed right alongside gifts like healing, prophecy, and tongues. The Greek word used here — kybernesis — refers to the act of steering, as a helmsman directs a ship. This imagery reminds us that administration is not just about getting things done — it's about helping ministries stay on course.

The gift of administration is Spirit-empowered. It is not limited to human ability. Like all spiritual gifts, it flows from the Holy Spirit, requires spiritual discernment, and bears Kingdom fruit. It is expressed through prayerful planning, Spirit-led structure, and God-inspired strategy. It is a supernatural grace given to build and edify the body of Christ.

To deny its spiritual nature is to miss the profound impact it can have when yielded to God.

Myth 3: Administrators Are Not Visionaries

Another common myth is that administrators are all about details and logistics but have no vision of their own. This assumption has led many to believe that administrators are only good at executing someone else's idea — that they are implementers, not initiators.

But the truth is that many administrators are deeply visionary. They may not always shout their ideas from the stage, but they see things others cannot. They have an eye for potential, a heart for purpose, and a mind for execution. Their vision is often expressed not through dreams alone, but through frameworks, structures, and systems that turn ideas into impact.

Nehemiah, again, is a powerful example. He wasn't simply carrying out someone else's plan — he had the burden, he caught the vision, and he led the charge. He saw what needed to be done and mobilised a nation to do it. His vision was strategic. His plans were spiritual. His leadership was administrative — and it changed the course of history.

Administrators are not limited to someone else's dream. They can dream too — and build the roads that lead others there.

Myth 4: Administration Is Restrictive

There's a belief in some circles that administration and structure are enemies of the Holy Spirit — that too much planning will quench the move of God. This fear is rooted in the false dichotomy that freedom and form cannot coexist.

But the Bible tells a different story.

God is not the author of confusion (1 Corinthians 14:33). The Spirit brings clarity, not chaos. Throughout Scripture, we see divine order facilitating, not hindering, the presence of God.

When Jesus fed the five thousand, He didn't just start handing out food randomly. He instructed the people to sit in groups (Mark 6:39–40), creating an organised environment for a miracle to take place. In Acts 2, after the Holy Spirit was poured out at Pentecost, Peter stood and brought explanation, order, and leadership to the moment. The outpouring didn't end in confusion — it led to structure, baptism, and community.

Administration is not a cage for the Spirit. It is a container. It does not limit revival — it sustains it. Good administration helps protect what God is doing. It ensures that what starts in the Spirit doesn't fall apart due to a lack of stewardship.

True freedom is not the absence of form — it is the result of good structure.

Myth 5: Anyone Can Do It

Because administrative work often looks practical, some assume that anyone can do it — that all it takes is a little organisation or effort. But this is like saying anyone can preach, pastor, or prophesy. It overlooks the fact that administration, too, is a spiritual calling.

The gift of administration carries a divine grace. Those called to it often experience a deep sense of fulfilment in organising people and resources. They thrive in complexity. They are calm under pressure. They find joy in planning and executing with excellence. They are spiritually wired to build systems and solve problems.

When people are placed in administrative roles without the gift or calling, they often experience burnout and frustration. They may become overwhelmed, miss details, or lack the foresight needed for growth. But when administrators are operating in their anointing, everything changes. Ministry becomes smoother. Leaders feel supported. Teams function with clarity and unity.

Just as not everyone is called to be a teacher or evangelist, not everyone is called to administrate. And that's okay. But for those who are — it is vital that they are recognised, empowered, and released.

Overcoming the Misconceptions

These myths have done real damage — not only to individual administrators but to churches as a whole. When administration is misunderstood, its potential is limited. When administrators are boxed in or undervalued, they retreat. And when churches resist structure, they often find themselves exhausted, disorganised, or stagnant.

But there is hope.

As we renew our understanding, we can begin to reclaim the beauty and power of this gift. When we honour administrators for who they are — spiritual leaders, strategic thinkers, and vital contributors to the mission — we release them to flourish.

We bring them to the leadership table, not just to take notes, but to shape the direction. We give them voice and value. We affirm that their gift is just as sacred as preaching or worship. We free them to serve not from a place of burnout, but from a place of calling.

For those who have carried the weight of these misconceptions — let them go. You are not "just" anything. You are called. You are needed. And you are seen by God.

Final Thoughts

Misunderstanding the gift of administration has limited the potential of many ministries. Churches have struggled with growth, excellence, and sustainability — not because of a lack of prayer or passion, but because of a lack of structure.

But structure is not the enemy of the Spirit. It is a partner. It is a sacred container for God's glory to dwell and move.

To the administrators reading this: You are not invisible. You are not unnecessary. You are not "just doing the admin." You are a Kingdom builder. A vision carrier. A spiritual leader. Your spreadsheets are sacred. Your meetings are ministry. Your strategies are Spirit-led.

God has entrusted you with a unique gift — to organise what others dream, to build what others pray for, and to sustain what others begin. Your hands bring order. Your voice brings wisdom. Your presence brings peace.

The church needs your gift — not later, but now. Not in the background, but at the forefront. And as you continue to serve, lead, and build, may you do so with confidence, knowing that your gift is not only useful — it is essential.

The Administrator vs. The Visionary

In every healthy church, ministry, or organisation, two powerful forces are at work — the visionary and the administrator. They are both leaders in their own right, but they operate from different paradigms, with different tools, and often with different temperaments. One is future-focused; the other is task-focused. One dreams in colour; the other builds in blueprint. And when these two work in unity, the result is extraordinary.

But when misunderstood, these roles can clash. Tension arises. Visionaries feel boxed in; administrators feel overwhelmed. Projects stall. Communication breaks down. The body suffers not because of a lack of gifting, but because of a lack of collaboration.

This chapter explores the contrast and complement between these two vital roles. We'll uncover how their differences can become strengths, and how working in partnership can transform not only organisations, but entire communities of faith.

Understanding the Roles

Let's start by defining each role more clearly.

The Visionary is the dreamer. They are often passionate, future-oriented, and innovative. Visionaries think big. They are captivated by possibility, stirred by what could be. They tend to see in broad strokes — major themes, bold ideas, compelling missions. They can envision a preferred future long before the path is clear.

But visionaries can struggle with details. They may leap from idea to idea without building a roadmap. They can sometimes overwhelm teams with enthusiasm but offer little clarity on how to implement what they imagine.

The Administrator is the builder. They are strategic, organised, and solution-focused. Administrators don't just hear vision — they translate it into action. They ask: What will this require? Who needs to be involved? What resources are needed? What's the timeline? They ensure that the dream is not just discussed, but delivered.

However, administrators can sometimes get stuck in systems. They may resist last-minute changes, struggle with ambiguity, or prioritise process over spontaneity.

Each role carries leadership weight. One is not more spiritual or important than the other. But each needs the other to flourish.

Biblical Examples of Visionary–Administrator Partnerships

The Bible is rich with examples of visionaries and administrators working together to advance the Kingdom:

> Moses and Joshua – Moses received the vision to lead the Israelites out of Egypt. He cast the vision, performed miracles,

and established the law. Joshua, his successor, took that vision and implemented it — leading the people into the Promised Land through strategy, structure, and courage.

David and Solomon – David dreamed of building a temple for God. He drew up the plans, gathered resources, and envisioned the glory of God dwelling among His people. But it was Solomon who executed the plan, overseeing the construction and organisation of the project to completion.

Paul and his teams – Paul had a powerful apostolic calling. He carried the vision to reach the Gentiles, plant churches, and write much of the New Testament. But his ministry succeeded because of administrators and co-labourers like Timothy, Titus, Phoebe, and others who managed the logistics, supported the churches, and kept the mission moving.

These examples show us that God often pairs dreamers with doers. The visionary may see the promised land, but the administrator helps the people get there.

When Visionaries Lead Alone

Vision is a gift — but without administration, it can become a burden.

Visionary leaders who operate without administrative support often face predictable challenges:

- Overcommitment – They say "yes" to too many things and spread themselves thin.
- Burnout – Without structure or delegation, they try to do everything themselves.
- Unfinished projects – Great ideas start strong but never reach completion.
- Disillusioned teams – Passion without process can lead to frustration and disengagement.

In the wilderness, Moses tried to lead alone — judging every dispute and carrying the entire weight of the nation. It took Jethro's counsel to show him a better way: share the load, appoint leaders, and implement structure (Exodus 18). Passion needs a plan. Inspiration without implementation exhausts everyone involved.

When Administrators Lead Alone

On the other hand, administrators without visionary leadership can also face pitfalls.

- Over-reliance on structure – Systems become the goal instead of serving the mission.
- Resistance to change – Fear of disrupting order can prevent innovation.
- Focus on maintenance over growth – The organisation becomes efficient but stagnant.
- Loss of purpose – Without vision, even the best systems lose meaning.

The Pharisees, in Jesus' day, were experts in structure. They had procedures for everything — but lacked the vision and heart of God. They missed the Messiah standing before them because they were too focused on the system.

The most beautifully structured church will decline if it lacks fresh direction. Administrators need visionaries to bring inspiration and forward movement.

Working in Partnership

When visionaries and administrators work together with mutual respect and shared purpose, the result is synergy.

Together, they can:

Craft compelling mission statements and develop action plans.

Launch new ministries with strategic timelines and achievable goals.

Maintain momentum while avoiding chaos or burnout.

Adapt to change without losing clarity or direction.

This partnership requires humility. Visionaries must recognise that their ideas are not threatened by structure. Administrators must remember that systems should serve people, not control them.

Healthy partnership sounds like:

The visionary saying, "I need your help to make this real."

The administrator saying, "I believe in the vision. Let's build a plan."

When these roles embrace each other, ministries move from inspiration to impact.

Communication Is Key

Much of the tension between visionaries and administrators comes down to communication. These roles think and speak in different languages:

Visionaries tend to speak in metaphors, ideas, and big-picture dreams. They assume others can fill in the gaps.

Administrators prefer specifics, timelines, and clearly defined outcomes. They want to know who's doing what, by when, and with what resources.

If left unaddressed, these differences can cause misinterpretation:

Administrators may feel overwhelmed or dismissed.

Visionaries may feel misunderstood or constrained.

Effective communication starts with listening. Visionaries must learn to slow down and clarify. Administrators must learn to listen for the heart behind the vision. Both must be willing to ask questions, give feedback, and affirm each other's contributions.

It helps when visionaries share not only the what but also the why. It helps when administrators respond not with resistance but with solutions. It helps when both sides remember: we're not on opposite teams — we're building the same Kingdom.

Embracing Your Role

Not everyone is wired to be a visionary. Not everyone is gifted to administrate. That's the beauty of the body — we are designed to need each other.

If you're a visionary:

Don't isolate yourself. Invite administrators into your process early.

Be willing to adjust your timeline or idea based on wise counsel.

Communicate your vision clearly and repeatedly.

Celebrate the administrators who make your dreams sustainable.

If you're an administrator:

Don't be afraid to ask for clarity. Vague ideas aren't disrespect — they need shaping.

Offer structure without shutting down creativity.

Keep communication open and constructive.

Celebrate progress and recognise the impact of your work.

And if you happen to be both — a rare but valuable combination — steward both gifts carefully. You may need help balancing your visionary impulses with your administrative responsibilities. Don't be afraid to ask for support.

A Story of Collaboration

Let's imagine a church that wants to start a food pantry ministry.

The visionary sees the big picture — feeding the community, partnering with other organisations, creating a space of love and dignity for the hungry.

The administrator asks, "What's the budget? Who will manage distribution? Where will we store the food? How do we track needs and inventory?"

At first, the questions may feel like resistance — but they're not. They're the beginning of implementation. Together, they build a team, develop a system, secure a location, recruit volunteers, and begin serving families every week.

This ministry thrives because vision and strategy co-exist. Dreams become discipleship. Passion finds a plan.

Final Thoughts

The body of Christ functions best when every part plays its role with excellence and humility. Visionaries and administrators are not rivals — they are co-labourers. One provides momentum; the other provides direction. One initiates; the other executes.

When churches learn to honour both — to celebrate the dreamers and the doers — they become unstoppable. Ideas no longer stay stuck in notebooks. They come to life. Ministries no longer fizzle out. They flourish. Leaders no longer burn out. They build.

God is not calling us to competition — He's calling us to collaboration. The Kingdom is advanced when passion meets process, when vision meets structure, and when people stop striving to do it all alone.

So whether you are a visionary or an administrator, do your part — and do it well. The church needs your gift. The world needs your impact. And the Kingdom needs your faithfulness.

You don't have to do everything. But when you do what you were created to do — and honour those around you who do the same — you'll help build something that lasts.

Church Administration in the 21st Century

The role of church administration has undergone a radical transformation. What once may have been viewed as a supportive, behind-the-scenes task has emerged as one of the most strategic and visible leadership functions in the modern church. The 21st-century church operates in a world that is fast-paced, highly connected, and increasingly complex. From technological advances to shifting cultural landscapes, today's church leaders must navigate more than spiritual dynamics — they must respond to legal, social, digital, and operational challenges.

This doesn't mean the spiritual essence of the Church has changed. The Gospel remains timeless. But how the Church functions in the world has evolved. And if churches are to thrive in this generation and beyond, the gift of administration must rise to meet the moment.

In this chapter, we'll explore the evolving role of church administrators and why they are critical to the health and relevance of the 21st-century Church.

The New Reality

Gone are the days when church administration was limited to printing bulletins, maintaining attendance records, and managing the church calendar on a wall. Today's church administrator must be multifaceted — part strategist, part technologist, part operations manager, and part team developer.

Modern administrators are now expected to manage:

- Online giving systems and donation tracking
- Virtual meetings and hybrid team coordination
- Data protection and compliance with government regulations (e.g., GDPR, UK Charity Commission requirements)
- Social media communication and public relations
- Volunteer onboarding and digital discipleship tracking
- Software and tech platforms for church management, event planning, and livestreaming

In essence, today's administrator is no longer working in the background — they are at the centre of church operations. Their insight and leadership shape how churches connect with their members and the wider world. The ability to remain spiritually anchored while managing multiple complex systems is what sets the 21st-century administrator apart.

Leading in a Digital Age

Digital transformation has redefined how churches gather, communicate, and disciple. The 2020 global pandemic accelerated the need for online engagement, and churches that once hesitated to adopt digital tools suddenly found themselves in a crash course on livestreaming, Zoom meetings, and virtual giving.

For administrators, this shift wasn't temporary — it was a new normal.

Churches now rely on administrators to manage:

- Livestreaming infrastructure (e.g., camera systems, streaming software, audio-visual teams)
- Digital event registration for services, classes, and conferences
- Email marketing systems and automated follow-up for guests and members
- Church Management Software (ChMS) to track giving, attendance, ministry involvement, and spiritual growth
- Online learning platforms for Bible studies, leadership training, and spiritual formation

Administrators must not only be tech-savvy themselves but also capable of training staff and volunteers to use these tools effectively. More importantly, they must ensure that technology serves the mission — not the other way around.

Data Stewardship and Compliance

In the digital age, churches collect and store a great deal of sensitive information — names, addresses, financial contributions, prayer requests, pastoral counselling notes, volunteer applications, and more.

This data must be handled with integrity, confidentiality, and compliance. Church administrators must now be fluent in:

- Data protection laws such as GDPR (General Data Protection Regulation)
- Cybersecurity practices to protect against data breaches or fraud
- Ethical record-keeping and consent policies
- Compliance reporting to governmental or denominational bodies

- Digital backups and contingency planning for emergencies

What was once a "nice to have" is now a legal and ethical necessity. Mismanagement of data can lead to reputational damage, legal action, and — most importantly — a breakdown in trust with the congregation.

Faithfulness in administration now includes being a faithful steward of information.

Ministry Models Are Changing

Church is no longer defined by Sunday morning alone. The rise of micro-churches, house gatherings, multi-site campuses, online-only congregations, and bi-vocational leadership models reflects a broader reimagining of what "church" can look like.

This shift has huge implications for administration.

Modern administrators must be prepared to:

- Build flexible systems that adapt to hybrid models of church
- Support multi-site coordination, including venue booking, tech support, and team rotation
- Develop leadership pipelines for smaller, more agile gatherings
- Create communication platforms that connect people beyond the Sunday experience
- Facilitate collaboration across time zones, countries, and cultures in global or diaspora communities
- The administrator of the future is someone who embraces decentralisation, supports innovation, and ensures that core systems — vision, care, discipleship, and communication — remain consistent across platforms and locations.

Volunteers in the Modern Church

Today's volunteers are different from those of previous generations. They are often:

- Busier with work and family obligations
- Less willing to commit long-term
- More engaged when they feel valued and empowered
- Motivated by purpose, not just participation

This shift requires a new approach to volunteer engagement. Effective administrators now:

- Streamline onboarding and training through digital platforms
- Offer short-term or project-based roles for those with limited availability
- Use automated scheduling systems to reduce miscommunication
- Develop feedback loops and regular check-ins
- Create culture-shaping practices like volunteer appreciation, team prayer, and leadership development

Volunteers are the lifeblood of most churches. A well-designed administrative system empowers them to serve with joy, confidence, and clarity.

Embracing Innovation with Discernment

In a world obsessed with novelty, not every new idea or tool deserves a place in the church. But neither should the church shy away from innovation out of fear. The administrator's role is not to jump on every trend, nor to dismiss all change — it is to exercise discernment.

Before adopting a new platform, ask:

- Does this help us disciple people more effectively?
- Does it improve communication or reduce barriers to ministry?
- Is it scalable and sustainable for our context?
- Will it enhance or hinder community and worship?
- Does it align with our values and theology?

Administrators are gatekeepers. They protect the church's integrity while guiding it toward greater effectiveness. Their decisions shape how the church engages its culture without compromising its calling.

Honouring the Past, Leading into the Future

One of the great tensions in modern church administration is managing change in communities where tradition runs deep. Many churches include long-time members who cherish familiar systems, liturgies, and routines. Change can feel threatening.

Wise administrators don't bulldoze tradition. They build bridges.

This involves:

> Sensitivity – Listening to concerns, affirming the value of what has come before
>
> Clarity – Clearly communicating why change is happening and how it serves the mission
>
> Inclusivity – Designing systems that allow everyone, regardless of age or background, to participate and flourish

In some cases, legacy systems may need to be retired. In others, they can be upgraded or reimagined. In all cases, administrators must navigate change with pastoral care and strategic wisdom.

Churches that manage this tension well often experience renewed unity and fresh momentum.

A Vision for 21st-Century Church Administrators

The administrator of the 21st century is no longer just the organiser in the background. They are the architect of systems, the bridge between departments, the integrator of vision, and often the first line of response in a crisis.

They carry both spiritual sensitivity and operational skill.

They speak the language of spreadsheets and the language of the Spirit.

They walk with both wisdom and innovation — honouring what God has done, while preparing for what God will do next.

This new era requires administrators who are:

> Prayerful – Seeking God for strategy, not just solutions
>
> Proactive – Anticipating needs and preparing accordingly
>
> Adaptable – Willing to change and grow in a rapidly shifting world
>
> Relational – Building trust, empowering teams, and leading with grace
>
> Faithful – Committed to excellence, integrity, and Kingdom values in every task

Administrators are not simply keeping the church running — they are helping it evolve, innovate, and remain faithful in a dynamic culture.

Final Thoughts

The 21st-century church is being called into deeper relevance, greater flexibility, and stronger foundations. This is not a time for fear — it is a time for faithful innovation. It is a time for Spirit-filled, strategic leaders to rise up and lead with clarity, competence, and conviction.

If you are a church administrator — or if you feel called to become one — know this: your role is vital. Your work is not invisible to God. Your leadership is shaping the future of the Church.

You are not just managing systems — you are stewarding revival.

You are not just scheduling volunteers — you are creating spaces for people to encounter Jesus.

You are not just responding to change — you are helping lead it with faith, wisdom, and strength.

This is your moment.

The Church needs administrators who can navigate complexity with grace. Who can marry structure with Spirit. Who can hold both the sacred and the strategic in tension — and lead the Church into her future with courage and hope.

Your hands build more than plans. They build legacy.

So step forward. Lead boldly. Serve joyfully. And innovate wisely — for the glory of God and the growth of His Church.

The Remote Church – Administration in a Digital Age

The COVID-19 pandemic didn't create the digital church — but it did fast-track its arrival. In just a few months, what was once considered optional or supplementary became essential. Livestreamed services, Zoom prayer calls, virtual small groups, and digital giving became standard operating procedures for churches worldwide.

Now, years later, the remote church isn't a temporary fix. It's a permanent feature of modern ministry life.

This new digital reality presents both incredible opportunities and unique challenges. And at the centre of it all is the gift of administration. Church administrators are now tasked with pioneering digital systems, managing online infrastructure, and ensuring the Church remains united, engaged, and Spirit-led — even when scattered across screens.

This chapter explores how administrators can lead confidently in this space, building connection, continuity, and clarity in an increasingly virtual world.

The Rise of the Remote Church

The shift to online ministry was once a reactive step. But it has since become a proactive strategy. Church is no longer confined to physical buildings or Sunday morning pews. It's on smartphones, laptops, and smart TVs. It's in group chats, livestreams, and YouTube channels.

Online church is not a Plan B — it's a primary environment.

And in this environment, administrators are vital.

They are now called to:

- Coordinate livestreams and digital worship experiences with excellence
- Manage multichannel communication across email, social media, and messaging platforms
- Design and implement remote workflows for staff, volunteers, and leaders
- Provide technical infrastructure and support, ensuring smooth virtual operations
- Oversee compliance and cybersecurity, protecting digital data and pastoral records

Without intentional digital administration, churches risk disconnection, disorganisation, and decline. With it, they have the tools to engage a broader, more diverse, and tech-savvy generation.

New Tools for New Times

Digital church leadership demands a new toolkit. Today's administrator must be comfortable with a range of platforms and technologies — and not just for their own use, but to empower the wider team.

Some essential tools include:

- Video conferencing platforms: Zoom, Google Meet, Microsoft Teams — for staff meetings, pastoral care, Bible studies, and small groups
- Church management software (ChMS): Planning Centre, Breeze, Elvanto, ChurchSuite — for organising people, ministries, and follow-up systems
- Digital giving platforms: Tithely, Givelify, PayPal, Stripe — for managing donations and financial tracking
- Collaboration tools: Trello, Asana, Notion, Slack — for project management, team communication, and shared task lists
- Livestreaming tools: OBS, ProPresenter, YouTube Live, Facebook Live, Restream — for reaching audiences with high-quality digital services

Administrators must become digital disciples — learning, training, and empowering others to use these platforms effectively. They are often the bridge between the vision and the technology that brings it to life.

The Power of Online Connection

One of the biggest misconceptions about digital ministry is that it leads to disconnection. While physical proximity is limited, relational connection is still possible — and necessary.

Administrators play a key role in designing intentional moments of connection across virtual environments. This includes:

- Regular online check-ins with volunteers, leaders, and team members
- Virtual welcome pathways for new guests, including digital forms, intro videos, and automated follow-up

- Online pastoral care, using messaging, video calls, or care request forms
- Hybrid events that include both in-person and online engagement

In a digital world, connection doesn't happen by accident — it must be engineered. Administrators help create systems that make sure no one is forgotten, even if they've never set foot in the building.

Challenges of Remote Administration

With great opportunity comes new obstacles. Remote ministry introduces a unique set of challenges that administrators must navigate with wisdom, patience, and foresight:

Communication Gaps

Without in-person interaction, messages can be missed or misunderstood. Administrators must develop strong communication rhythms, using tools like weekly email updates, group chats, and virtual team huddles.

Volunteer Fatigue

Online ministry can sometimes feel transactional. Volunteers may feel disconnected, underappreciated, or stretched thin. Administrators need to build systems of support, celebration, and encouragement.

Technical Barriers

Not everyone is tech-savvy. Some church members or leaders may struggle to adopt digital tools. Providing training, tutorials, and tech teams can bridge the gap.

Discipleship Shallowing

Online content is easy to consume passively. Administrators must work with ministry leaders to ensure engagement pathways — such as interactive Bible plans, discussion groups, and accountability partnerships — are in place.

Challenges are real — but so are the solutions. The administrator's foresight and flexibility can turn barriers into bridges.

Developing Digital Systems for Spiritual Growth

Church is more than a livestream. It's a community. It's discipleship. It's transformation. Digital ministry must not only reach — it must also form.

Administrators are instrumental in building systems that prioritise spiritual growth in a virtual environment. These systems may include:

Online discipleship tracks: Courses or small group pathways hosted through Zoom, Google Classroom, or learning platforms

Automated follow-up: Email sequences or text messages for newcomers, including devotional resources and next steps

Virtual service planning: Coordinating speakers, worship teams, tech, and media elements for cohesive online gatherings

Spiritual accountability tools: Prayer request databases, mentoring pairings, or check-in forms for pastors and leaders

These systems don't replace the Holy Spirit — they make room for Him to move more effectively. A church that is both spiritual and structured can grow deep and wide — even online.

Leading Remote Teams

Remote teams are a defining feature of the digital age. Whether paid staff or volunteer leaders, many ministry teams now operate from different locations. The old model of gathering around a conference table must evolve into a rhythm of virtual collaboration.

Administrators can lead the way by:

Setting clear goals, deadlines, and expectations

Using cloud-based tools (like Google Drive or Dropbox) to ensure documents and plans are accessible

Hosting weekly check-ins to track progress, provide support, and pray together

Cultivating team culture with virtual games, testimonies, appreciation shout-outs, and online devotionals

Remote doesn't mean distant. It means distributed. And with the right structures, distributed teams can be just as unified and effective as those under one roof.

Embracing Hybrid Ministry

The future of church is not either digital or physical — it is hybrid. Administrators must now think in terms of dual engagement, creating seamless experiences that serve people both in person and online.

This includes:

- Designing events that offer both physical attendance and livestream access
- Coordinating digital registration for on-site activities
- Collecting and analysing data across platforms to measure engagement, attendance, and growth

- Developing systems for follow-up that are inclusive of both online guests and in-person visitors
- Ensuring that discipleship, care, and communication span both spaces

Hybrid church is not a compromise — it's an expansion. It allows churches to reach further, serve wider, and disciple deeper. And administrators are the architects of that expansion.

The Digital Mission Field

The online world is not just a tool — it's a mission field. Billions of people spend hours online each day, searching for meaning, connection, and hope. The Church must not retreat from this space — it must invade it with purpose.

Administrators have a vital role in this digital mission:

- Facilitating consistent, high-quality content creation and distribution
- Creating onboarding funnels that help online visitors move toward deeper community
- Building partnerships with content creators, designers, and digital marketers
- Supporting pastors and ministry leaders in digital evangelism and outreach strategies

Just as missionaries once crossed oceans to share the Gospel, today we cross algorithms, platforms, and pixels. The tools have changed, but the mission is the same.

Final Thoughts

We are living in an unprecedented time — one that is full of change, disruption, and opportunity. The Church has not been sidelined by the digital age; it has been given a new platform to share timeless truth.

The gift of administration is more vital than ever.

You are not simply adapting — you are advancing. You are not just managing screens and software — you are stewarding revival in a new space. You are not just solving problems — you are paving new paths for the Gospel.

As the Church becomes more digitally present and globally connected, administrators will be the ones holding it together with grace, strategy, and spiritual sensitivity. You are building bridges — between people, between platforms, and between heaven and earth.

So lean into your role. Learn the tools. Train the teams. Build the systems. Protect the mission.

You are not behind the scenes. You are at the heart of it.

This is not just remote work — this is Kingdom work.

Keep building. Keep innovating. Keep trusting the One who has called you.

Because the Church needs administrators like you — now more than ever.

The Administrator's Role in Church Growth

Church growth is often celebrated in terms of numbers — more salvations, more members, more services, more impact. And while the spotlight is often placed on dynamic preaching, vibrant worship, or effective outreach, these visible aspects are only one side of the story. Behind the scenes, often unnoticed, are administrators laying the foundation that enables sustainable growth.

True church growth — the kind that produces long-term fruit and not just momentary excitement — cannot happen without strong, Spirit-led administration. It is the administrators who build the scaffolding for growth, design the pathways for connection, and protect the systems that nurture discipleship.

This chapter explores the essential role administrators play in enabling, sustaining, and scaling church growth. Because the truth is simple: growth without order leads to collapse. But growth with administration leads to transformation.

Growth Needs Infrastructure

Churches are often praying for growth, but when the growth comes, they are not always prepared to manage it. Without adequate infrastructure, growth can overwhelm a church. New people come in, but there's no system to connect them. Ministries expand, but no one knows who's doing what. Volunteers increase, but there's no clear path for training or communication.

This is where administrators shine.

Administrators understand that enthusiasm is not enough — structure must support momentum. As the church grows, administrators are responsible for building systems that ensure people are not lost in the crowd, volunteers are not overburdened, and ministries do not collapse under their own weight.

Key areas that require intentional administrative structure include:

- Visitor follow-up – digital forms, databases, and automated touchpoints
- Next steps – systems that help people move from "attendee" to "participant"
- Volunteer pathways – onboarding, role descriptions, and team rotations
- Discipleship tracks – small groups, mentorships, Bible classes
- Internal communication – calendars, updates, and coordination across departments

Without these systems, growth creates confusion. With them, growth leads to fruitfulness.

Biblical Principles for Organised Growth

The early church encountered the same challenges. In Acts 6, the church was experiencing explosive growth. But that growth revealed a weakness: widows were being overlooked in the daily distribution of food. This was not just a logistical issue — it was a spiritual opportunity.

Rather than ignoring the problem or asking the apostles to work harder, the church responded with administrative wisdom. Seven capable men were appointed to oversee the food distribution — men who were known for being full of the Spirit and wisdom. This wasn't just delegation. It was strategic, Spirit-led administration.

And what was the result?

"The word of God spread. The number of disciples in Jerusalem increased rapidly..." (Acts 6:7)

When administrative leadership was strengthened, the church grew faster and stronger. The same is true today. When churches recognise and empower administrators, they remove bottlenecks, improve care, and increase capacity.

The Pipeline to Discipleship

Church growth isn't just about attracting crowds — it's about making disciples. And discipleship doesn't happen by accident. It happens through intentional, Spirit-led systems.

Administrators play a key role in designing what we can call the pipeline to discipleship — the process by which a person moves from first-time visitor to mature follower of Christ.

Key components of a discipleship pipeline include:

- Digital connection cards – that integrate with Church Management Software (ChMS)

- Follow-up emails and calls – scheduled and tracked with accountability
- Volunteer onboarding – with training resources and clear communication
- Small group coordination – matching people with leaders and measuring attendance
- Mentorship and leadership development – through progress tracking and personalised check-ins

The smoother the pipeline, the more likely people are to engage deeply. When people know where they are, what's next, and who's walking with them, they grow. And it's administrators who make this clarity possible.

Managing Growth Seasons

Growth often comes in waves. A big Easter service. A citywide outreach. A viral social media post. A powerful revival weekend. These moments bring in new people and new energy. But they also bring pressure.

Without solid administration, churches risk:

- Losing track of new visitors
- Overworking existing volunteers
- Scheduling conflicts between ministries
- Overlooking key follow-up opportunities
- Experiencing burnout among leaders and teams

Wise administrators anticipate these seasons. They don't just respond to growth — they prepare for it. They work in advance to:

Ensure data collection systems are ready

Schedule extra volunteer support

Reserve spaces for follow-up gatherings

Prepare printed materials or digital resources

Coordinate team debriefs and evaluations

In the parable of the nets (Luke 5:4–7), the disciples had to repair and strengthen their nets before the miraculous catch of fish. In the same way, administrators strengthen the nets of the church to hold the harvest God is bringing.

Three Pillars Administrators Strengthen

Let's explore three key pillars that administrators help build and maintain to support church growth:

1. Sustainability

A growing church is exciting, but it must also be sustainable. Administrators ensure that:

- Systems are not built around a single personality but can be maintained over time
- Volunteers are trained, rotated, and appreciated to avoid burnout
- Resources — financial, human, and physical — are used wisely and replenished regularly

Sustainable churches are not the ones that run the fastest — they're the ones that keep running faithfully.

2. Scalability

What works for 50 people doesn't always work for 500. Administrators think ahead. They ask:

- Can this system grow with us?
- What needs to change at the next level of capacity?

- Where are our bottlenecks and how do we solve them?

Scalability ensures that ministries don't hit a ceiling. Instead, they expand with grace and intention.

3. Stability

Growth often brings change. Pastors may transition. New ministries launch. Crises may emerge. Administrators provide stability in these seasons by:

- Documenting processes and maintaining continuity
- Keeping the church calendar and budget aligned
- Offering consistent leadership when others feel overwhelmed

In a storm, stability matters. Administrators provide that anchor.

The Ministry of Stewardship

At its core, administration is about stewardship. Jesus taught that those who are faithful with little will be entrusted with much (Luke 16:10). Administrators are stewards of:

- Time – creating efficiencies and reducing wasted effort
- People – ensuring individuals are cared for, empowered, and released into ministry
- Facilities – managing the logistics of space, bookings, and maintenance
- Finances – budgeting, forecasting, and ensuring wise Kingdom investment
- Information – protecting data, tracking growth, and enabling informed decisions

Each of these areas can either propel or hinder church growth depending on how they're managed. Faithful administrators steward these areas with diligence, prayer, and excellence — not for their own sake, but for the sake of the mission.

Case Study: The Follow-Up Funnel

Imagine this: A church hosts a powerful Easter service and 250 people attend for the first time. The service is excellent — the worship is moving, the sermon is strong, and the response is encouraging.

But what happens next?

Without administration:

- Visitor cards are lost or forgotten
- No follow-up emails or texts are sent
- Leaders don't know who came
- Guests feel unseen and don't return

With administration:

- Visitor info is entered into a database within 48 hours
- A personalised welcome email and video are sent the next day
- Volunteers call or text within a week
- Guests are invited to a "Newcomers' Lunch" and guided into small groups or next steps

The result? Connection, care, and retention.

It wasn't just the Sunday service that made the impact — it was the system that followed. This is the power of administration. It catches the fish, not just for the moment, but for the mission.

Final Thoughts

Church growth is ultimately the work of God — "He gives the increase" (1 Corinthians 3:7). But just as God asked Noah to build the ark, Moses to structure the camp, and the disciples to prepare the nets, God expects us to be ready for what He's about to do.

Administrators are the ones who build the nets. They prepare the ground. They make room.

If you are an administrator, never forget this: your work is deeply spiritual.

Your spreadsheets are sacred.

Your workflows are worship.

Your planning meetings are preparation for revival.

When God sends the increase, your systems will be what hold it. When new people come, your follow-up will be what welcomes them. When disciples grow, your structure will be what supports them.

Keep building. Keep stewarding. Keep believing.

The harvest is coming — and the Church will need what you've prepared.

Challenges Administrators Face in the Church

Church administrators serve at the unique and often complex intersection of ministry and management. They are planners in a prophetic environment, system builders in a Spirit-led culture, and detail keepers in a world fuelled by divine vision. Their work is foundational to the health, stability, and growth of the church — yet they often carry heavy responsibilities with little visibility or acknowledgment.

While every role in the church comes with its challenges, the nature of administrative leadership creates unique pressures that can lead to discouragement, frustration, burnout, and even spiritual isolation if not recognised and addressed.

In this chapter, we will explore some of the most common — and often silent — challenges church administrators face. More importantly, we'll look at how these challenges can be navigated with wisdom, faith, support, and resilience.

1. The Overlooked Gift

One of the deepest and most painful struggles for many administrators is feeling unseen or undervalued. Because administration tends to happen behind the scenes, it is often assumed to be less impactful or spiritual than more public-facing ministries like preaching, worship leading, or evangelism.

Administrators may hear things like:

"You're just the organiser."

"That's not ministry — it's admin."

"We need more anointing, not more structure."

"Anyone can do that."

These words, even when said without malice, can deeply wound someone who has been called and anointed to serve through administration. Over time, these experiences can create self-doubt, low morale, and a reluctance to offer input or step into leadership moments.

But Scripture is clear: every part of the body matters — and often the most vital parts are the ones we don't see.

"On the contrary, those parts of the body that seem to be weaker are indispensable… But God has put the body together… so that there should be no division in the body, but that its parts should have equal concern for each other." (1 Corinthians 12:22-25)

Administrators may work in the shadows, but they carry light. Their gift is not "just admin" — it's leadership. And when affirmed, encouraged, and empowered, it becomes a force for incredible transformation.

2. Lack of Clear Authority

Many administrators are responsible for systems and people but lack the formal authority to lead decisively. They are expected to oversee processes, maintain order, and implement structure — yet their input may be dismissed or overridden by ministry leaders who have more visible authority.

This imbalance can result in:

- Tension with pastors or team leads
- Frustration when policies are ignored
- Confusion about decision-making roles
- Burnout from bearing responsibility without adequate support

The solution isn't to create hierarchy for its own sake — it's to establish clarity and alignment.

Every church administrator needs:

- A clear job description with defined responsibilities
- Decision-making boundaries that are respected
- Support from pastoral leadership, especially when introducing change
- Access to meetings and planning conversations where decisions are made

Empowerment begins with clarity. Administrators function best when they're not guessing what's expected or navigating mixed signals from leadership.

3. Resistance to Change

Change is necessary for growth, but it is rarely easy — especially in churches with long-standing traditions, cultures, or structures. Administrators are often tasked with introducing new systems, updating processes, or streamlining ministry workflows. And with that responsibility comes resistance.

People may push back for many reasons:

- Fear of losing control
- Attachment to "how things have always been done"
- Skepticism about the need for change
- Fatigue from previous failed initiatives

This resistance can feel personal, even when it's not. Administrators may feel defeated, unappreciated, or misunderstood.

To navigate this challenge, administrators must:

Lead with patience, recognising that change is a process, not an event

Communicate the "why" behind the change clearly and repeatedly

Demonstrate the value through small wins and measurable outcomes

Involve stakeholders early, inviting feedback and collaboration

Over time, resistance can soften when people see results and feel included. Change led with grace creates cultures of growth.

4. Spiritual Misunderstanding

One of the more subtle — but deeply painful — challenges administrators face is the belief that their work is less spiritual than other forms of ministry. This myth often goes unspoken, but it shows up in:

A lack of prayer covering for administrative leaders

Exclusion from spiritual leadership discussions

Comments that imply their work is "secular" or "business-like"

This disconnect creates an internal tension:

Am I truly called to this?

Does God value what I do?

Why does this feel so important, but seem so invisible?

The truth is, administration is deeply spiritual. Scripture is full of examples:

Nehemiah rebuilt the city walls with strategy and prayer.

Joseph managed a national crisis with integrity and wisdom.

The deacons in Acts 6 solved a food distribution problem and unlocked growth in the early church.

God doesn't separate the sacred from the structured. He moves in order, rhythm, and divine systems. Administrators are part of how He leads His Church.

5. Emotional and Mental Fatigue

Administrative work may appear calm on the outside, but it often involves:

- Constant problem-solving
- Unrelenting detail management
- People issues
- Crisis response
- Deadline pressure

When combined with the spiritual weight of ministry, this can lead to:

- Emotional exhaustion
- Mental overload
- Anxiety or perfectionism
- Feelings of inadequacy

Over time, administrators may begin to question their calling or lose their sense of joy in serving.

The answer is not to "push through" — but to practice wise self-care:

- Schedule sabbath rest
- Set healthy boundaries around availability
- Learn to delegate and empower others
- Spend intentional time in prayer, Scripture, and worship — not just planning

A rested administrator is a resilient one. And your soul matters just as much as your systems.

6. Navigating Difficult People

Churches are full of wonderful people — and some challenging ones. Administrators often find themselves in the middle of conflicting personalities, competing priorities, or communication breakdowns.

Whether it's:

A ministry leader who resists deadlines

A volunteer who disregards procedures

A staff member who won't respond to emails

A church member who doesn't understand boundaries

...administrators are often the ones caught in the tension.

This requires:

> Emotional intelligence – understanding what's really going on beneath the surface
>
> Clear communication – speaking truth in love, with consistency
>
> Conflict resolution training – knowing when to mediate and when to escalate
>
> Pastoral support – not being left alone to handle hard situations

Difficult people are part of ministry — but they don't have to derail it. Administrators thrive when they're equipped for healthy relationships, even in tough moments.

7. Underfunded and Undervalued

It's not uncommon for churches to invest heavily in what's seen — lighting, sound systems, stages — while neglecting the systems that support what's unseen. As a result, administrators often face:

- Outdated or limited technology
- Insufficient budgets for tools and platforms
- Lack of training resources
- Pressure to "make do" rather than grow

This creates frustration and sends a subtle message: "Your role is not a priority."

But administrators can advocate for change by:

- Articulating the value of administration in terms of mission outcomes
- Presenting data that shows how systems support discipleship, giving, or growth

- Suggesting scalable solutions — starting small but aiming for strategic investment
- Demonstrating excellence, even with limited resources

Over time, excellence attracts investment. When administrators lead with faith and fruit, others begin to see the value they bring.

Encouragement for the Journey

The challenges administrators face are real — but so is the calling. The gift of administration may be misunderstood by some, but it is not overlooked by God.

God sees your late nights and early mornings.

He honours your spreadsheets, your checklists, your phone calls.

He delights in the order you bring, the peace you protect, and the paths you prepare.

Every form you process, every meeting you coordinate, every plan you build — it's all part of His mission. You are doing Kingdom work. You are not just supporting ministry — you are doing ministry.

Final Thoughts

Administrators carry a sacred calling. Yes, they face unique pressures. But they also have unique grace.

If you're an administrator:

Know your worth. You are not invisible to God.

Set healthy boundaries. You can't lead well if you're running on empty.

Find your tribe. Connect with other administrators for support and prayer.

Speak up. Share your insights, your challenges, and your vision with confidence.

Stay close to the Spirit. You are not alone — you are led, empowered, and anointed.

Challenges are part of the calling, but they do not define it. You are called for such a time as this — and the Church needs your strength, your wisdom, and your leadership.

Stay faithful. Stay prayerful. Stay grounded in your purpose.

You are not "just an administrator." You are a builder of God's house. And your work is holy.

Taming the Wild Horse – Nurturing the Gift of Administration

The gift of administration, like many spiritual gifts, comes with immense potential — both for good and for challenge. Administrators are often natural leaders: highly capable, detail-oriented, and driven by a desire to bring clarity, order, and excellence. They see problems others don't. They plan, organise, and execute with precision. Their minds are wired for systems; their hearts beat for efficiency and effectiveness.

And yet, this strength — when not nurtured, refined, and surrendered to the Holy Spirit — can become a double-edged sword. What is meant to bring peace can bring pressure. What should build unity can unintentionally create division. What is designed to serve can begin to control.

In this chapter, we explore what it means to tame the wild horse — to bring our administrative gift under the lordship of Christ so that it serves the Church with grace, humility, and love. Because when the administrator grows, the whole church benefits.

The Untamed Administrator

Every strength has a shadow. And the administrator's greatest strengths — decisiveness, precision, leadership, clarity — can, if unchecked, turn into:

- Controlling tendencies
- Frustration with slower-paced people
- Perfectionism
- Relational breakdowns
- Resistance to visionary or pastoral leadership

An untamed gift may look like:

- Taking over tasks without being asked
- Correcting people publicly to maintain order
- Implementing systems without consulting those who will use them
- Struggling to delegate because no one "does it like I do"
- Dismissing creativity in favour of control

These behaviours don't stem from bad intentions. They often come from zeal — a genuine desire to see things work well. But when passion overrides process, or when systems become more important than people, the gift begins to hurt rather than help.

The goal is not to suppress that strength, but to submit it to the Spirit. Like a wild horse, the administrative gift is most powerful when it is guided, not when it runs wild.

The Power of Mentorship

One of the greatest catalysts for growth in any administrator's journey is mentorship.

Administrators — especially those who are highly competent — may be prone to working alone. They may assume that productivity equals maturity. But skill and character are not the same. Just because an administrator can get the job done doesn't mean they're growing in grace.

A mentor provides:

> Loving accountability – speaking truth, even when it's hard to hear
>
> Spiritual perspective – helping connect administrative work to Kingdom purpose
>
> Relational insight – offering feedback on tone, timing, and delivery
>
> Emotional wisdom – helping process frustration, rejection, or burnout

Mentorship turns raw talent into refined leadership. It helps the administrator discern not only what needs to be done, but how to do it in a way that honours God and values people.

No administrator is too experienced for input. Growth doesn't stop with competence — it continues with character.

Servant Leadership

At the heart of healthy administration is a posture of servant leadership.

Jesus, the greatest leader the world has ever known, modeled leadership through service. He washed feet. He carried burdens. He corrected with compassion. He saw people, not just outcomes.

For administrators, servant leadership means:

- Prioritising relationship over results
- Leading with gentleness and patience
- Supporting team members, not just managing them
- Waiting on God's direction, not just relying on their own logic

- Remembering that people are not problems to be solved, but souls to be shepherded

True leadership is not about control — it's about care. Administrators who serve like Jesus will find that their influence expands, not because they demand authority, but because they cultivate trust.

Emotional Intelligence in Leadership

Administrators often deal with multiple people, departments, and expectations. And while systems may seem predictable, people are not. To lead effectively, administrators must develop emotional intelligence — the ability to understand and manage both their own emotions and those of others.

Key areas of emotional intelligence include:

Self-awareness – recognising one's triggers, strengths, and blind spots

Self-regulation – responding calmly under pressure instead of reacting

Empathy – discerning what others are feeling, even when they don't say it

Social skill – navigating group dynamics, listening well, and communicating clearly

Adaptability – adjusting one's leadership style to suit different personalities

For administrators, emotional intelligence enables them to move from simply managing tasks to leading people. And leadership, at its core, is relational. It's not just about what we do — it's about how we do it.

Spiritual Discernment

While administrators are known for logic and structure, they must also cultivate spiritual discernment. Ministry doesn't run on systems alone — it runs on the guidance of the Holy Spirit.

Discernment helps administrators:

- Know when to act and when to wait
- Discern the season the church is in — growth, rest, change, or consolidation
- Sense when a decision feels right strategically but wrong spiritually
- Prioritise people over plans when needed
- Lead with prayer, not just preference

A Spirit-led administrator is powerful. They bring both wisdom and timing to the table. They know how to plan — but they also know when to pause, when to pivot, and when to pray.

Discernment transforms good administration into godly administration.

Creating Space for Growth

Administrators grow best when they are given room to learn, freedom to fail, and support to reflect. This requires intentional leadership from pastors, elders, or other leaders who are committed to their development.

Ways to support administrators include:

Creating clear job scopes and expectations

Providing regular feedback that affirms and challenges

Offering training opportunities in leadership, communication, and conflict resolution

Encouraging spiritual formation through retreats, mentoring, or sabbath rhythms

Reminding them that they are not machines — they are ministers

Growth happens not when we are pushed harder, but when we are shepherded well. Churches that invest in their administrators will find that their ministries run with greater excellence, longevity, and unity.

When the Administrator Grows

A nurtured and discipled administrator becomes:

- More gracious – patient with those who process or respond differently
- More collaborative – inviting input rather than insisting on control
- More discerning – sensitive to both spiritual and emotional needs
- More Spirit-led – trusting God's timing, not just their own timelines
- More empowering – raising others up rather than doing everything themselves

They still carry strength — but it is sanctified strength. It no longer bulldozes people or dominates meetings. Instead, it builds bridges, carries burdens, and strengthens teams.

Their leadership becomes magnetic — not because they force things into place, but because they create space for others to flourish.

Final Thoughts

The gift of administration is like a wild horse — strong, powerful, and capable of great movement. But left untrained, it can become chaotic, stubborn, or even dangerous. Taming that wild horse does not mean breaking its spirit. It means shaping it for greater purpose.

If you are an administrator:

> Don't be afraid of growth.
> Don't resist feedback.
> Don't isolate yourself in your own systems.

Instead:

> Embrace mentorship.
> Pursue humility.
> Lead with servanthood.
> Rely on the Holy Spirit, not just your spreadsheet.

You were not created to control — you were called to cultivate.

You were not called to prove your worth — you were chosen by God to carry order, clarity, and excellence into His Church.

So let Him refine you. Let others shape you. And let your gift be a blessing, not just a strength.

The Church doesn't just need administrators who can get things done. It needs administrators who are Spirit-filled, people-focused, and Christ-like in every way.

Because when you grow, the whole body grows.

The Gift of Administration in the Secular Workplace

The gift of administration is often associated with church offices, Sunday service logistics, or ministry events. But what if its reach is far greater? What if administration is not just for the church — but for the world?

Many administrators are called to serve in secular environments — schools, hospitals, corporations, local councils, non-profits, and even government agencies. These spaces, though not overtly spiritual, are nonetheless fields of influence. They are places where the order, wisdom, and integrity of God can shine through the work of His people.

In this chapter, we explore how the gift of administration operates outside of the church and how Christian administrators can honour God in the workplace, carry Kingdom values into professional settings, and use their administrative gift to shape culture, systems, and lives.

Recognising Your Calling Beyond the Church

Many Christian administrators feel a divide between their "spiritual life" in church and their "professional life" at work. They may see their role in the secular world as simply a means of provision, while their real ministry happens in the evenings or on weekends.

But this is a false divide.

God doesn't separate the sacred from the secular — He integrates them.

The same spiritual gift that organises Sunday services can also run Monday morning meetings. The same wisdom that builds church systems can design business operations. The same integrity that oversees church finances can transform corporate budgeting.

God's calling doesn't switch off at the office door.

Biblical examples abound:

- Daniel served in the courts of Babylon, administrating for multiple kings with prophetic wisdom and integrity.
- Joseph managed the storehouses of Egypt, building a national infrastructure that saved millions.
- Esther influenced royal administration from within, using her access and discernment to save a nation.

These were not "ministry settings" — yet their work was deeply spiritual. And so is yours.

Characteristics of Spirit-Led Administrators at Work

The gift of administration — when surrendered to the Spirit — carries characteristics that stand out in any environment. Christian administrators in the secular workplace often reflect:

1. Integrity
They make honest decisions even when no one is watching. They don't cut corners, manipulate numbers, or play politics.

2. Discernment
They understand timing, process, and people. They bring insight to meetings, foresee potential issues, and quietly avert crises.

3. Excellence
Their work is thorough, well-planned, and efficient. They don't just meet expectations — they exceed them.

4. Peacefulness
They remain calm under pressure. In chaotic teams or high-stress environments, their presence is grounding.

5. Order
They bring clarity where there is confusion, direction where there is drift, and systems where there is disarray.

These qualities often lead to increased trust, influence, and leadership — even without a title or formal recognition.

Their leadership may not always be overtly spiritual — but it reflects the character of Christ.

Bridging Faith and Professionalism

One of the challenges Christian administrators face is how to live out their faith authentically in a professional environment where explicit religious expression may not be welcome or appropriate.

But this is where subtle, Spirit-filled influence comes into play.

You don't need to preach in the breakroom or quote Scripture in your reports to make an impact. Instead, let your ethics and excellence speak:

Let your integrity make others curious about your values.

Let your consistency point people to your source of peace.

Let your grace under pressure become a witness to God's presence.

Paul writes in Colossians 3:23:

"Whatever you do, work at it with all your heart, as working for the Lord, not for human masters."

That means your work is worship.

Your meeting notes can honour God.

Your project timeline can reflect His order.

Your kind leadership can model His love.

Your decision-making can express His wisdom.

You are not a secular worker — you are a spiritual ambassador in a secular setting.

Overcoming Challenges in Secular Spaces

While working in the marketplace is a powerful calling, it doesn't come without tension. Christian administrators often face unique pressures, including:

1. Value Conflicts

You may be asked to bend the truth, fudge numbers, or support practices that contradict your convictions. These moments require courage, clarity, and, sometimes, sacrifice.

2. Faith Isolation

You might feel like the only Christian in the room — which can lead to spiritual loneliness or discouragement.

3. Pride and Positioning

In highly competitive environments, it can be tempting to seek influence through self-promotion rather than servanthood.

4. Balancing Authority and Humility

You may hold leadership positions, but you're still called to lead like Christ — with humility and service, not dominance.

How do you stay strong?

Stay grounded in prayer. Start your day with God, even if your day is filled with meetings.

Stay connected to other believers — whether in your church, a Christian workplace fellowship, or online communities.

Keep short accounts with God — bring your frustrations, fears, and failures to Him.

Remember your why. You are not just doing a job. You are advancing the Kingdom through your excellence.

Case Study: Faith in the Boardroom

Sarah, a Christian administrator in a large financial corporation, led several high-profile projects involving millions in assets. She couldn't openly evangelise in her environment, but she approached her work with prayer, diligence, and honesty.

THE GIFT OF ADMINISTRATION

She built trust quickly by delivering projects on time, mediating team tensions with wisdom, and refusing to compromise on ethics — even when pressured.

One day, a colleague confided, "You always have a calm about you. You don't panic. You're fair. What drives you?"

Her response wasn't rehearsed. It wasn't even deeply theological.

She simply said, "I follow Jesus. I try to reflect Him in how I work and lead."

That colleague eventually began asking more questions, attending a church event, and exploring faith.

Sarah didn't preach from a pulpit. She didn't post verses on the wall. But her life preached every day — through the way she worked.

That's the power of administration as witness.

When the Church Equips the Marketplace

Often, church teaching focuses on Sunday ministry roles — preaching, worship, prayer — and overlooks those called to the marketplace. But the church has a responsibility to affirm and equip marketplace administrators as ministers in their own right.

Practical ways churches can support administrators in the workplace:

- Teach a theology of work — showing how secular work can be sacred
- Host forums and small groups for Christian professionals
- Create mentorship pathways between church leaders and workplace leaders
- Pray publicly for those in secular leadership roles
- Encourage testimonies of workplace ministry and witness

Administrators in the workplace are missionaries. They may never stand on a church stage, but they stand in boardrooms, classrooms, staff meetings, and civic spaces carrying the presence of God.

When churches champion these administrators, the ripple effect touches every sphere of society.

Bringing Kingdom Culture to Corporate Culture

Christian administrators have a unique opportunity to influence culture — not by enforcing religion, but by embodying Kingdom principles.

Ways to bring Kingdom culture into your workplace:

- Create systems that serve people, not just profit
- Lead teams with dignity, giving every voice value
- Resolve conflict with grace and humility
- Celebrate others and foster a culture of encouragement
- Model Sabbath and rest, even in fast-paced settings
- Pray silently but powerfully for your co-workers, your leaders, and your organisation

You may not change the entire culture overnight — but you can be a seed of transformation. You can bring light to leadership, peace to pressure, and excellence to execution.

Final Thoughts

The gift of administration is not limited by context. It is limitless in purpose. Whether you're leading in a church office or managing a team in a global corporation, your gift matters — and it's holy.

You are not a second-class minister because your desk is not in a sanctuary.

THE GIFT OF ADMINISTRATION

You are not spiritually inferior because your meetings involve spreadsheets instead of sermons.

You are sent. You are strategic. You are sacred.

So work with purpose. Lead with grace. Build with integrity.

Let every system you streamline, every team you organise, and every decision you steward be an offering to God.

Because His plan for your gift goes beyond the building — it touches cities, industries, cultures, and nations.

Let your faith fuel your excellence — and watch God use your administration to change the world.

Case Studies and Lessons from Real Church Administrators

Theology gives us foundation. Strategy gives us direction. But testimony? Testimony brings truth to life.

Throughout this book, we've explored the biblical, spiritual, and practical dimensions of the gift of administration. But sometimes, what encourages us most isn't more theory — it's the real-life stories of people just like us. People who have sat at the same desks, juggled the same responsibilities, navigated the same tensions — and found grace, growth, and fruitfulness along the way.

In this chapter, we share stories from administrators across different contexts, cultures, and denominations. Some serve large urban churches, others lead in small rural settings. Some are volunteers; others are full-time staff. Each one is unique — but all share a common truth: administration, when stewarded with faith and wisdom, builds lasting ministry.

Let their stories inspire and instruct you. Let them remind you that you are not alone — and that your work, though often unseen, is deeply significant in the Kingdom of God.

Case Study 1: Bringing Order to Chaos

Maria – Full-time Administrator, Urban Church

Maria was hired as the first full-time administrator for a rapidly growing church in the heart of the city. When she arrived, the church was bustling with activity — but behind the scenes, it was disorganised. There was no central calendar. Volunteer teams overlapped or forgot their commitments. Events were planned last-minute, and Sunday services often ran late due to miscommunication.

At first, Maria felt overwhelmed. "There was energy and excitement," she recalls, "but it was like building a house with no blueprint." Instead of criticising, she began gently introducing change. She implemented a church-wide scheduling system, set up regular planning meetings, and designed a monthly operations review.

Within six months:

Services flowed smoothly.

Volunteers felt equipped and empowered.

Pastoral staff experienced reduced burnout.

Church attendance increased by 20%, not because of a new programme, but because people experienced peace and consistency.

Lesson: Order creates space for revival. Behind-the-scenes organisation is not the opposite of the Spirit — it makes room for Him to move.

Case Study 2: Shepherding through Systems

James – Associate Pastor & Administrator, Mid-sized Church

James had a heart for discipleship, but he noticed something troubling: people were falling through the cracks. New members weren't being followed up. Small group leaders felt disconnected. Discipleship was more of a hope than a plan.

With permission from his lead pastor, James spent two months building a new system:

A digital CRM to track member engagement

Monthly check-ins with small group leaders

A growth pathway that included Bible classes, service opportunities, and mentorship

What followed was transformation:

Small group participation rose by 40%

More than 60 people completed discipleship classes

Leaders began to spot and develop new leaders from within their groups

James said, "I realised that systems don't replace shepherding — they support it."

Lesson: Systems are pastoral. When built with love and prayer, they can help shepherd people more effectively than we imagine.

Case Study 3: The Quiet Culture-Changer

Jola – Volunteer Administrator, Multicultural Church

Jola wasn't in a paid role. She didn't have a ministry title. But she had a heart to serve — and a keen eye for details.

She began by organising the church's files. Then she introduced a simple event checklist for leaders. Eventually, she built a hospitality schedule and designed a welcome pack for new visitors.

Three years later, her church — once described as "passionate but scattered" — became known as one of the most hospitable churches in the area. Visitors consistently commented on how warm, well-structured, and welcoming the experience was.

Most people didn't know Jola was behind the systems. And she didn't mind. "I just wanted people to feel at home," she said. "And I knew that order could create that space."

Lesson: You don't need a title to make a difference. Influence doesn't require a microphone — just faithfulness.

Case Study 4: Resisting Burnout with Boundaries

Jonathan – Operations Director, Large Multi-site Church

Jonathan was excellent at what he did. He managed multiple campuses, oversaw dozens of volunteers, and was the go-to person for almost everything operational. But it came at a cost. He worked late most nights. Weekends were always on-call. His family was feeling the strain, and so was his faith.

"I loved the mission," Jonathan said, "but I was starting to resent the work."

After confiding in a mentor, he made some tough but necessary changes:

- He restructured his calendar to include rest and personal devotion.
- He empowered other leaders by delegating responsibilities.
- He instituted shared decision-making among his team.
- He implemented Sabbath principles, even within a high-demand setting.

Within a few months, his energy returned. His marriage strengthened. His staff felt more trusted. And he found a renewed love for the church.

Lesson: Healthy administration begins with a healthy administrator. Boundaries are not barriers — they are wisdom in action.

Case Study 5: Turning Around a Declining Ministry

Linda – Consultant Administrator, Rural Church Network

Linda was called in to assess a regional youth ministry that had plateaued. Participation had dropped, communication between churches was unclear, and leaders were discouraged.

Her audit revealed several core issues:

- Overlapping roles with no clarity
- An outdated communication system
- Events that were planned but poorly followed up

Over nine months, Linda led the team through a transformation:

- Clear role descriptions were created
- A digital dashboard helped coordinate communication
- Event feedback forms were introduced to guide future planning
- Youth leaders were trained in volunteer management and follow-up strategy

By the end of the year:

- Participation had increased by 25%
- Leaders reported feeling unified and energised
- A new wave of young leaders had stepped up

Lesson: Administration revives what feels stagnant. Sometimes what seems like a spiritual slump is really a structural one.

Case Study 6: Navigating Transition

Alan – Interim Administrator, Denominational Office

Alan was asked to serve as interim administrator for a church that had just lost its senior pastor. The staff were uncertain. The congregation was anxious. Programmes were in limbo.

Rather than launching something new, Alan stabilised what was already in place:

He ensured payroll, communications, and service planning continued without disruption.

He created a simple internal FAQ to keep the congregation informed.

He scheduled regular staff prayer times to bring peace and unity.

Six months later, when the new pastor arrived, they found a church that was not in disarray — but ready to move forward.

Lesson: Stability is ministry. Administrators provide the calm in the chaos, helping churches transition without trauma.

Collective Themes and Takeaways

While the settings differ, each of these stories underscores foundational truths for administrators:

Faithfulness beats fanfare. You may never be applauded — but your work will bear fruit.

Structure serves the Spirit. Systems do not hinder revival; they make room for it.

Leadership is quiet strength. You don't have to shout to lead — you just have to show up, consistently.

Health matters. You can't build strong ministries from a burnt-out place. Rest is part of your calling.

You are not alone. Others have walked this path — and there's a community of builders just like you.

Final Thoughts

Your story might not be written in this chapter — yet. But it's being written every time you open your laptop to organise the calendar. Every time you pray over a project plan. Every time you stay late to ensure the church runs smoothly on Sunday. Every time you remind a team that their work matters.

You are a story of faithfulness.

You are not just a background helper — you are a builder of God's house.

Let these testimonies be a reminder: God sees you.

When you feel tired — He strengthens.

When you feel unseen — He remembers.

When you feel unsure — He equips.

So keep building. Keep leading. Keep administrating.

Your spreadsheets are sacred. Your systems are worship. Your diligence is discipleship. And your legacy is eternal.

Navigating Leadership Conflicts

No matter how Spirit-filled a church is or how well-designed the systems are, conflict among leaders is inevitable. Wherever people work together — especially in emotionally charged, vision-driven environments like ministry — misunderstandings, tension, and disagreement are bound to arise.

Church administrators, who often serve as the connective tissue between departments, teams, and leadership structures, frequently find themselves in the middle. They may not initiate conflict, but they often carry the fallout — mediating conversations, correcting course, and helping keep the ministry moving forward.

This chapter explores the administrator's role in navigating leadership conflict with wisdom, grace, and emotional intelligence. Conflict doesn't have to lead to division. Handled well, it can lead to clarity, maturity, and stronger unity.

Understanding the Nature of Conflict

Conflict in itself is not inherently negative. In fact, conflict can be productive when it sharpens understanding, challenges assumptions, or reveals areas that need growth. The Bible is full of examples:

Paul and Barnabas disagreed so sharply over John Mark that they parted ways (Acts 15:36–40). Both continued in fruitful ministry — and later, Paul even affirmed Mark's usefulness (2 Timothy 4:11).

Moses and Aaron dealt with murmuring and rebellion, both among the people and within their leadership circle.

Even the disciples argued over who was greatest in the Kingdom (Luke 22:24).

What matters is not the presence of conflict — it's the response to conflict. Will we retreat, escalate, ignore, or resolve? Will we prioritise ego or unity?

Administrators, when grounded in their calling, can help turn tension into testimony.

Where Administrators Fit In

Administrators may not always be the decision-makers in church leadership — but they are often the connectors:

They manage systems that touch every team.

They often interact with both pastoral and operational leaders.

They are tasked with implementing decisions — which means they experience the gaps and tensions in real-time.

They serve as a sounding board for frustrated volunteers or overwhelmed staff.

Their position allows them to see across departments and understand relational dynamics that others may miss. This gives them a unique vantage point — but also a vulnerable position.

The administrator must learn how to:

Navigate neutrality without becoming passive.

Offer perspective without becoming political.

Preserve peace without sacrificing truth.

They are called to be bridge-builders, holding space for both clarity and compassion.

Common Leadership Tensions

Let's name a few of the most frequent leadership conflicts that administrators encounter:

1. Vision vs. Implementation

Visionary leaders often want to move fast, break new ground, or follow inspiration on short notice. Administrators, by nature, think in terms of structure, process, and timelines. The tension arises when visionaries feel "slowed down" and administrators feel "steamrolled."

2. Role Confusion

Unclear job descriptions, overlapping responsibilities, or shifting authority lines can lead to frustration, especially when decisions are made without including key people.

3. Communication Gaps

Missed emails, unclear expectations, or assumptions can spiral into personal offense. Administrators may be blamed for "not keeping everyone informed," even if decisions weren't communicated to them in the first place.

4. Personality Clashes

Some leaders are direct, others are diplomatic. Some are emotional processors, others are facts-first. Administrators are often caught between strong personalities with very different styles.

5. Volunteer vs. Staff Dynamics

Paid staff may have different expectations, time commitments, or accountability structures than volunteers — yet they often work on the same teams. This can cause resentment or inconsistency if not carefully managed.

The Administrator's Approach: Wisdom in Action

Rather than taking sides or retreating in fear, administrators are called to lead relationally, even without the final authority.

Here are practical ways administrators can help resolve and prevent conflict:

1. Listen to Understand

James 1:19 reminds us to be "quick to listen, slow to speak, and slow to become angry." Active listening uncovers heart issues behind surface tensions. It allows leaders to feel heard and builds trust.

2. Ask Clarifying Questions

Don't assume you understand the issue. Ask questions like:

"What do you need that you feel you're not receiving?"

"Where do you see the breakdown occurring?"

"Have you shared this directly with them?"

These questions encourage reflection, not reaction.

3. Clarify Roles and Expectations

Often, conflict stems not from bad motives but from unclear assumptions. Administrators can help:

- Review job descriptions
- Confirm decision-making authority
- Schedule regular communication rhythms

Structure prevents strain.

4. Model Matthew 18

When tension arises, Jesus instructs us to go directly to the person involved (Matthew 18:15–17). Encourage peers or team members to have face-to-face (or screen-to-screen) conversations before involving leadership unnecessarily.

5. Facilitate Mediation

In cases where personal conversations fail or the conflict is complex, administrators can recommend mediation — either by organising a meeting with a neutral party or involving senior leadership to guide the process.

When You're in the Middle

One of the most difficult positions to be in is when the administrator becomes the messenger, mediator, or middleman in a leadership conflict. These moments require emotional strength and spiritual clarity.

Here are some tips for surviving and thriving in the middle:

Stay neutral: Avoid gossip or venting. Protect your integrity.

Keep records: Document decisions, conversations, and expectations clearly to avoid misunderstandings later.

Clarify your role: Don't take on responsibilities or emotions that don't belong to you.

Seek pastoral covering: If you feel torn, ask for guidance and prayer.

Maintain your peace: Spend time with God. Don't let unresolved tension steal your joy or shake your calling.

The Heart of a Peacemaker

Jesus said, "Blessed are the peacemakers, for they will be called children of God" (Matthew 5:9). Not peace-keepers — peacemakers. Those who actively build bridges where there are divides.

For administrators, that means cultivating:

1. Humility

Not every argument needs your input. Choose your battles. Be willing to listen more than you speak.

2. Wisdom

Know the difference between what is urgent and what is important. Understand timing — sometimes the best intervention is delayed until emotions settle.

3. Courage

Conflict avoidance is not leadership. Sometimes, the most loving thing you can do is to gently bring the issue into the light.

4. Prayerfulness

There's a spiritual dimension behind every relational breakdown. Pray before meetings. Intercede for your leaders. Ask God to show you what's really going on.

A Testimony: Healing Through Honesty

Moyo, a church administrator in a multicultural congregation, noticed ongoing tension between the worship director and the youth pastor. Events were being double-booked. Announcements were missed. The youth team felt ignored, while the worship team felt micromanaged.

Rather than choosing a side, Moyo scheduled a shared planning meeting and acted as facilitator. She began the session by affirming both teams and then invited each leader to share, uninterrupted, what they were experiencing.

The results were surprising:

> Both leaders realised they shared similar values.
>
> They discovered that a simple calendar oversight had created months of confusion.
>
> They agreed on a monthly sync-up meeting to ensure alignment.

Today, their ministries not only collaborate — they champion one another.

Lesson: The administrator didn't solve the problem by imposing a fix — she created space for honesty and reconciliation.

Preventing Conflict Through Systems

Prevention is better than cure. Many conflicts arise not from malice but from miscommunication. Administrators can create systems that reduce the likelihood of friction:

- Shared calendars and project boards
- Clear documentation of roles and responsibilities
- Team charters outlining values and expectations
- Feedback loops where staff can share concerns early
- Annual reviews that include relational as well as performance check-ins

Healthy systems support healthy relationships.

Final Thoughts

Leadership conflict isn't always comfortable — but it is inevitable. And it is not a sign of failure. In fact, when handled with humility and wisdom, it can become a powerful catalyst for growth, clarity, and unity.

As an administrator, you are not just a systems person. You are a steward of peace.

You create room for understanding.

You hold space for reconciliation.

You help build a culture where hard conversations are possible — and even welcomed.

Your role in conflict resolution is not always glamorous or easy. But it is profoundly Kingdom-impacting.

So be a bridge. Be a listener. Be a peacemaker.

And trust that as you do, God is working through you to build a church that reflects His wisdom, His unity, and His love.

Building Effective Teams with the Right Leadership Structures

A church's effectiveness is shaped not only by the power of its preaching or the passion of its worship, but also by the health of its leadership teams. No matter how visionary a church is, or how much faith is present, poor team dynamics and unclear structures can hinder growth, weaken morale, and lead to burnout.

Conversely, when leadership teams are aligned, structured, and supported, the church becomes not only spiritually vibrant but also organisationally sound. Ministries run smoothly, communication flows, and people experience a sense of belonging and purpose.

Administrators are uniquely positioned to play a central role in this process. While they may not always be in the spotlight, they are often the architects of structure, the facilitators of systems, and the stewards of team health. They help ministries move from chaos to clarity and from inspiration to execution.

In this chapter, we explore what makes a strong leadership team and how administrators can help design and sustain the structures that allow those teams to thrive, grow, and serve with excellence.

Why Structure Matters

Some may argue that structure stifles the Spirit. But the Bible consistently shows us that structure supports the Spirit. From creation's ordered rhythm to the detailed blueprints of the tabernacle, God is a God of design and intentionality.

In the context of leadership, structure provides:

- Clarity – so everyone knows their role and responsibilities
- Accountability – so decisions and actions are measured and shared
- Continuity – so ministries outlive transitions and crises
- Efficiency – so energy is spent on people, not confusion
- Momentum – so leaders can focus on mission instead of managing dysfunction

Without structure:

- Responsibilities become blurred
- Communication becomes fragmented
- Conflict becomes inevitable
- Leaders become exhausted

With healthy structure, churches experience:

- Better alignment across departments
- Stronger collaboration between leaders
- Greater trust among volunteers and staff
- More consistent fruit and sustainable growth

Administrators are often the ones who design, implement, and maintain these structures — ensuring that vision doesn't stay stuck in planning mode, but moves forward with purpose.

Biblical Models of Teamwork

Scripture gives us several powerful models of team building that highlight the importance of clarity, delegation, and shared responsibility:

1. Moses and the Elders (Exodus 18)

When Moses was overwhelmed by the weight of leadership, his father-in-law Jethro advised him to appoint capable men over groups of thousands, hundreds, fifties, and tens. This created layers of leadership and empowered others to share the load.

Lesson: Effective teams multiply leadership through delegation.

2. Nehemiah's Work Crews (Nehemiah 3)

Nehemiah assigned families and leaders to rebuild specific sections of the Jerusalem wall. Everyone had a clearly defined part to play, and the work was completed in just 52 days.

Lesson: Strong teams have specific assignments with shared ownership.

3. Jesus and the Twelve (Luke 6:13)

Jesus didn't attempt to disciple the world alone. He selected twelve leaders, invested in them, gave them authority, and later sent them out in pairs. They were His team — and later became the foundation of the early Church.

Lesson: Even Jesus built a team and trusted them to carry the mission.

Each of these models includes defined roles, delegated responsibility, and spiritual oversight — essential ingredients in effective team design.

Components of a Healthy Team Structure

Administrators can help churches and ministries move from informal groups to intentional teams. Below are foundational components that contribute to healthy team structure:

1. Defined Roles and Responsibilities

Ambiguity breeds anxiety. Every team member should know:

- What they are responsible for
- Who they report to
- What success looks like in their role

When roles are clear, teams experience confidence, autonomy, and collaboration — not competition.

2. Mutual Accountability

Healthy teams don't just answer to the senior leader — they also hold each other accountable. This fosters mutual respect and shared ownership. Administrators can implement tools like:

- Peer reviews
- Regular one-on-ones
- Anonymous feedback loops
- Ministry performance dashboards

Accountability should feel supportive, not punitive — a tool for growth, not guilt.

3. Shared Vision

A team without a shared vision will eventually drift in different directions. Administrators can help ensure that:

- Ministry plans reflect the overall mission of the church

- Calendars are aligned to avoid scheduling conflict
- Budgets are structured around strategic goals
- Goals and outcomes are tracked and celebrated

When everyone pulls in the same direction, progress is faster — and more joyful.

4. Rhythms of Communication

Clear and consistent communication is the lifeblood of effective teams. Administrators can help:

Schedule regular staff or ministry meetings

Document decisions and send follow-ups

Track action items and follow-through

Build shared digital platforms for collaboration (e.g., Slack, Trello, Google Drive)

Communication rhythms prevent misalignment and build relational trust.

5. Leadership Development Pathways

A healthy team is a growing team. Administrators can help identify gaps, raise new leaders, and implement growth plans, including:

- Training sessions or leadership labs
- Volunteer onboarding and orientation
- Mentorship pairings
- Succession planning

Development ensures that the ministry is not dependent on any one person — including the administrator.

Avoiding Common Pitfalls

As teams grow, challenges can emerge. Administrators are well-placed to spot and solve these issues before they become systemic problems.

Pitfall 1: Overlapping Roles

When two people believe they own the same task, confusion and competition arise. A clear ministry org chart can help delineate roles.

Pitfall 2: Bottlenecks

If every decision must be approved by one person, the team slows down. Empower leaders at different levels to make decisions appropriate to their role.

Pitfall 3: Volunteer Fatigue

When the same people are doing everything, burnout is inevitable. Administrators can schedule rotations, create rest periods, and implement recognition strategies.

Pitfall 4: Inconsistent Feedback

Without regular input, team members don't know if they're doing well — or how to improve. Implement consistent check-ins and reviews.

Building Teams with Vision and Values

Strong teams are not only structured around roles — they are built on shared values. A skillful team without shared values will eventually fracture. A value-aligned team, even with average talent, will thrive.

Administrators can help embed values such as:

Humility – We serve one another.

Excellence – We do our best with what we've been given.

Collaboration – We're better together.

Honour – We speak well of and to each other.

Flexibility – We hold our plans loosely when God leads differently.

Ways to reinforce values:

Include them in onboarding and orientation processes

Revisit them during team retreats, vision nights, or reviews

Model them in tone, language, and decision-making

Celebrate when values are demonstrated, not just when goals are achieved

Culture is formed not by what is printed on the wall, but by what is practised in the hallway.

A Real-Life Example: From Teams to Movement

Kendra, a church administrator for a church planting network, noticed that although each ministry had passionate leaders, there was constant overlap, tension, and miscommunication. Events were scheduled on the same weekends, volunteers were stretched thin, and budgets were duplicated.

She stepped in with permission from the lead pastors and began to:

Map out each team's responsibilities

Create a central planning calendar

Align each ministry's goals with the church's core mission

Introduce quarterly leadership huddles for communication and celebration

The result?

Interdepartmental unity grew

Volunteer satisfaction increased

Giving rose as members saw greater impact

The church launched two new campuses with confident teams and clear systems

Lesson: Structure didn't restrict ministry — it released it.

Final Thoughts

Strong teams are built — not born. They don't happen by accident. They require intentional leadership, prayerful oversight, and wise administration.

As an administrator, you are not just managing meetings or drawing charts. You are helping to create the relational and organisational ecosystem where ministry can thrive.

Your spreadsheets are sacred.

Your org charts are Kingdom blueprints.

Your team trainings are discipleship tools.

Your calendar is a prophetic alignment of purpose.

So keep building.

Keep clarifying.

Keep empowering.

The teams you are structuring today are the ministries of tomorrow. And through your gift of administration, the church can rise into maturity, unity, and lasting impact — all for the glory of God.

Beyond the Four Walls – Interest Groups and Community Impact

The mission of the Church was never meant to remain confined within a building. While gathering together in worship, teaching, and fellowship is essential to the life of the body, much of the transformative work of the Gospel happens beyond the four walls — in neighbourhoods, schools, marketplaces, cafés, homes, and online spaces.

The Church is not a location; it is a movement. And that movement needs administrative support to flourish.

This chapter explores the role of church administrators in equipping the Church to reach beyond Sunday, beyond programmes, and beyond its property lines — by supporting interest-based groups, organising community outreach, building strategic partnerships, and creating sustainable systems for mission that lasts.

Why Community Engagement Needs Administration

Outreach is often seen as spontaneous — and in some ways, it should be. Spirit-led compassion, quick responses to needs, and grassroots innovation are all beautiful. But without intentional planning and structure, even the most passionate outreach efforts can fall flat.

Without administration:

- Volunteers burn out due to unclear roles
- Resources are mismanaged or duplicated
- Follow-up is inconsistent or forgotten
- Impact is difficult to measure or improve

In contrast, when community engagement is undergirded with strong administration, the church becomes a well-prepared vessel for Spirit-led service.

Administration turns good intentions into lasting impact.

Administrators help ensure that what starts as a great idea doesn't die from disorganisation — but is nurtured into a thriving ministry with ongoing fruit.

Interest Groups: Where Ministry Gets Personal

One of the most effective ways to engage people beyond the sanctuary is through interest-based groups — small gatherings formed around shared passions, life stages, or challenges. These groups often attract people who may not be ready to attend a Sunday service, but who are open to relationship and support.

Types of interest groups may include:

- Parenting support groups
- Fitness and wellness meetups

- Entrepreneur and small business communities
- Youth and mentorship circles
- Creative arts collectives
- Grief or recovery groups

These groups are deeply relational. They meet people where they are, build trust through shared experience, and often become the entry point to deeper discipleship.

Administrators can play a vital role in launching and sustaining these groups by:

- Coordinating leader recruitment and training (including safeguarding and background checks)
- Scheduling meeting times and securing venues or rooms
- Creating registration and attendance systems
- Designing promotional content and communication templates
- Tracking group health, including growth, attendance, and next-step follow-ups

When structured well, these groups offer not only personal support but a bridge into the wider church community.

Ministry becomes accessible. Relationships become intentional. And growth becomes measurable.

Outreach That Multiplies

From food banks to school supply drives, from visiting care homes to community clean-ups — outreach is one of the clearest expressions of the Church's love in action.

Yet many outreach ministries struggle with:

- Inconsistent volunteer engagement
- Unclear communication
- Last-minute planning
- No follow-up or evaluation
- Untracked outcomes

Administration solves these problems. A strong outreach strategy includes:

1. Volunteer Management Systems

Recruitment, training, and clear role descriptions

Rotas and reminders to prevent no-shows

Debriefs and appreciation efforts to maintain morale

2. Logistics and Resource Allocation

Budget planning and procurement systems

Transportation, set-up, and contingency planning

Health and safety or liability considerations

3. Follow-Up Pathways

How will we stay in touch with people served?

What resources or invitations will we offer next?

How will we integrate those interested into discipleship?

4. Impact Tracking

How many people served?

What stories or testimonies emerged?

What partnerships were formed or strengthened?

What can we improve next time?

When administrators help build these systems, outreach becomes repeatable and scalable, rather than draining and chaotic.

Great outreach isn't about doing more — it's about doing it better, with lasting fruit.

Partnering with the Community

Some of the most powerful kingdom work happens when churches collaborate with others — schools, councils, local businesses, other churches, or non-profits.

Administrators are often the ones tasked with building and managing these external relationships, ensuring both the spiritual and legal sides of the partnership are in place.

Key administrative contributions include:

- Drafting memorandums of understanding (MOUs) or partnership agreements
- Ensuring safeguarding, insurance, and liability coverage
- Aligning schedules, goals, and budgets between stakeholders
- Managing shared projects or joint events
- Coordinating reporting and follow-up after collaboration

These partnerships can open doors to:

- Greater reach and visibility in the community
- Shared funding or resource opportunities
- A reputation of trust and integrity for the church

Administrators help move partnerships from verbal agreement to functional alliance.

A Missional Mindset

For administrators, community engagement is not just a task — it's a mission. A spreadsheet is not just a tool for scheduling; it's a means of serving people with excellence. A system isn't just a workflow; it's a structure that holds up Gospel ministry.

The mindset shift is this:

"I'm not just organising an event — I'm creating opportunities for people to encounter Christ."

This changes everything.

As administrators, ask:

Who is our community?

What needs are present around us?

Where are the relational bridges already being built?

How can our systems help people connect, grow, and belong?

With the right mindset, every event plan becomes a Gospel opportunity. Every follow-up call becomes a seed of faith. Every form or flyer or facility booking becomes part of the Kingdom's expansion.

A Real-Life Example: Transforming a Neighbourhood Through Order

Nathan, a part-time administrator at a mid-sized church, noticed that their annual back-to-school drive had great turnout but poor follow-up. They gave away backpacks, food, and clothes — but rarely saw those families again.

Nathan implemented several small but impactful changes:

- Digital sign-in with permission to follow up
- A thank-you text sent the next day with an invite to a parenting group
- Volunteer debriefs to reflect on the event's spiritual and logistical impact
- A rotating team of follow-up callers to invite families to church or kids' programmes

Within a year, nearly 20 families who first came for free backpacks had become active church members.

Lesson: Outreach without follow-up is like sowing seed without expecting a harvest. Good administration turns one-time moments into lifelong transformation.

Empowering Interest Group Leaders

Interest groups only succeed when they are led well. And leaders need support — not just encouragement, but infrastructure.

Administrators help create a healthy environment for group leaders by:

- Designing clear leadership expectations and guides
- Hosting monthly check-ins or leader huddles
- Equipping leaders with templates for communication or curriculum
- Offering care and prayer support, especially during seasons of difficulty
- Identifying emerging leaders for coaching or succession planning

Supporting leaders means the ministry doesn't just grow wide — it grows deep.

Preventing Burnout in Outreach

Many outreach ministries suffer from enthusiasm fatigue. What starts with excitement can quickly lead to discouragement, especially if:

Events are overwhelming to plan

The same few people do everything

Success isn't clearly measured or celebrated

Administrators can guard against this by:

Building annual outreach calendars in advance

Rotating team leads and volunteers to prevent overload

Using impact stories to encourage teams

Debriefing after events to assess what worked (and what didn't)

Creating a culture of celebration and rest

When systems serve people, outreach becomes a joy, not a burden.

Final Thoughts

The Church is called to be salt and light, not only inside the sanctuary but throughout the streets, schools, homes, and neighbourhoods around it. And in order for that calling to be fulfilled consistently and excellently, administration must be present.

Administrators are the ones who:

- Turn passion into programmes
- Turn ideas into action plans
- Turn one-time outreach into long-term impact
- Turn interest groups into discipleship communities

THE GIFT OF ADMINISTRATION

Your work may be behind the scenes, but its impact is far-reaching. You help the Church stretch beyond its walls and become what it was always meant to be: a people on mission.

So keep organising, planning, supporting, and refining. Keep building systems that serve the poor, uplift the broken, and welcome the curious.

Your gift is not just making the Church stronger — it's making the world better.

You are not just managing logistics. You are facilitating love in action.

16

A Call to Action – The Future of Church Administration

The Church is entering a new era. The world around us is changing at a pace we've never seen before — through technology, globalisation, generational shifts, and cultural upheaval. In the midst of all this, the mission of the Church remains unchanged, but the methods must adapt.

As ministry continues to evolve, one thing has become increasingly clear: the future of the Church depends not only on visionaries and pastors but on Spirit-filled administrators who can anchor vision in structure, lead with both strategy and discernment, and equip the Church for sustainable, impactful mission.

This chapter is a call to action. Whether you are a seasoned church administrator, a ministry leader with a gift for systems, or someone just discovering your administrative calling, this is your moment to step forward with boldness, creativity, and faith.

The future needs you.

What the Future Requires

The church of tomorrow will not be built on charisma alone. It will require collaboration, capacity, and courage. And administrators will be central to that foundation.

Administrators of the future must be able to:

1. Think Theologically and Strategically

You're not just a systems thinker — you're a Kingdom builder. Understanding theology and mission will help you design structures that reflect God's heart and honour His people.

2. Innovate While Honouring Tradition

Honouring legacy doesn't mean resisting change. The best administrators will bridge the past and the future, respecting what has worked while leading teams into what's next.

3. Lead with Skill and Humility

Technical competence must be balanced with spiritual maturity. Administrators will need both strong leadership skills and servant-hearted posture to guide teams, manage resources, and model Christ-like leadership.

4. Build Scalable, Sustainable Systems

Short-term fixes won't cut it. Churches need systems that grow with them — that work now and five years from now. Administrators must develop solutions that multiply ministry, not just maintain it.

5. Disciple Others into Administrative Ministry

The future doesn't belong to individuals — it belongs to teams. Administrators must learn to reproduce themselves, mentor emerging leaders, and raise up others who carry this gift with clarity and confidence.

Digital and Hybrid Ministry Models

As digital tools become fully integrated into how churches operate, the administrator's toolbox is expanding. Churches now livestream, use apps for giving, hold online discipleship groups, and manage databases of members across cities and nations.

Tomorrow's administrators must be:

Digitally literate – familiar with tools like ChMS (Church Management Software), project platforms like Trello or Asana, and communication tools like Slack, Zoom, and social media schedulers.

Ethically grounded – making wise decisions around data privacy, security, and digital discipleship.

Hybrid architects – designing seamless experiences that integrate both in-person and online engagement.

Data-informed – using analytics not to reduce people to numbers, but to understand needs, measure growth, and improve ministry impact.

Technology is not the mission — but it is now one of the Church's most powerful tools for mission. And administrators will help guide the Church in stewarding it well.

Multiplication Over Maintenance

In the past, administration was often viewed as maintenance — keeping the lights on, managing calendars, and fixing problems when they arose.

But the Church can no longer afford to simply maintain.

The future belongs to ministries that multiply — new leaders, new churches, new expressions of outreach and discipleship. Administrators must ask:

Are our systems ready for growth?

Can we replicate what we're doing in other locations or formats?

Who are we training to take our place?

Are we building something that will outlast us?

A multiplication mindset shifts the focus from "keeping things running" to building what can run without you — a legacy of leadership, systems, and sustainability.

Discipling the Next Generation

If administration is truly a spiritual gift, then it must be discipled like any other. Yet too often, young people with administrative gifts are redirected toward more visible roles — preaching, worship, or youth ministry — simply because administration is not understood or valued.

It's time to change the narrative.

Administrators must lead the way in:

- Mentoring young leaders who show aptitude for systems, logistics, or planning
- Creating internships and entry-level ministry roles that expose others to the gift of administration
- Celebrating administrative wins publicly, so others see the impact
- Speaking from the pulpit or platform about administration as a sacred calling
- Including administrators in leadership conversations, not just operations meetings

The Church must stop relegating administration to the sidelines and start treating it as a discipleship path and leadership track.

When young people see administration as a Kingdom calling, they will rise to carry it.

Advocacy Within the Church

For too long, many administrators have worked in silence — under-recognised, under-resourced, and under-utilised. But the future Church needs administrators who are not only skilled, but also courageous advocates for what's needed to serve well.

This is not about ego — it's about stewardship.

Administrators must begin to:

- Speak up for healthy systems that prevent burnout and support growth
- Advocate for better tools, training, and tech to empower ministry
- Set healthy boundaries that model sustainable service
- Teach teams the spiritual value of planning, structure, and order
- Challenge old mindsets that diminish or dismiss administrative work as "less spiritual"

When administrators own their calling, they give others permission to do the same.

Reimagining What's Possible

What if administration wasn't seen as a "necessary support role," but as a strategic leadership lane?

What if churches included administrators in senior leadership retreats — not just to take notes, but to shape strategy?

What if church planters had administrative co-founders from day one — someone to steward systems while they cast vision?

What if every worship team had an administrator who ensured communication, rehearsal schedules, and tech logistics were flawless?

What if every outreach team had a behind-the-scenes lead who ensured follow-up, data entry, and next-step integration happened?

That's the future of Church administration. It's not about filing papers. It's about facilitating revival.

The Call Is Now

This is a defining moment for the gift of administration. In the midst of global uncertainty, declining church attendance, and generational change — the body of Christ needs builders, planners, organisers, and strategists who can help the Church move with clarity, compassion, and conviction.

Administrators are not optional.

They are essential.

And their seat at the leadership table is not a favour — it is faithfulness to the full expression of God's gifts within His Church.

Final Thoughts

The future of the Church will be fast, flexible, and Spirit-led. But it will also require frameworks, systems, and structures to carry what God wants to do.

Administrators — your time is now.

Step forward with:

CALLED TO ORGANISE. ANOINTED TO SERVE.

Boldness – Your voice matters.

Creativity – Innovation is in your DNA.

Faith – God has graced you for this moment.

Worship – Let your spreadsheets and strategy be soaked in prayer.

Legacy – Build something that outlives you.

You are not just reacting to what's next — you are shaping it.

The Church needs you at the table. Not to take minutes, but to make decisions. Not to just serve the vision — but to strengthen and scale it.

So rise up, administrator. Not in the shadow — but in the Spirit.

Lead. Build. Guide. Multiply. Disciple.

This is your call to action.

And the future of the Church will be stronger because you answered it.

Preparing the Ground – Positioning the Gift for Greater Impact

As we've explored throughout this book, the gift of administration is not an afterthought — it is a divine strategy for building, sustaining, and multiplying ministry. Administrators carry a spiritual mandate to bring clarity where there is complexity, movement where there is stagnation, and order where there is potential.

But the journey doesn't stop with personal understanding. It must lead to preparation — not only for current effectiveness but for future multiplication.

This chapter marks a turning point. If the earlier chapters have laid the theological and practical foundations for honouring the gift of administration, what follows now must equip us to develop others in it.

Because if we stop with ourselves, we miss the greater calling: to raise up more administrators who are spiritually mature, mission-minded, and organisationally equipped.

Laying a Foundation for the Future

Churches, ministries, and Kingdom movements are built across generations. Every administrator, no matter their age or experience, must begin to think like a multiplier:

- Who am I training to carry what I carry?
- How can I pass on what I've learned?
- Where are the future leaders with this gift?
- What systems and culture will outlive my current role?

Administration is not simply about managing what is. It's about preparing the ground for what could be.

That means building:

- Systems that scale
- Teams that grow
- Structures that include succession
- Culture that values administrative leadership

The Shift from Manager to Multiplier

Many administrators are excellent at managing details and leading teams — but the next season requires something more: reproduction. Not just leading well, but raising up other leaders who carry the same heart, values, and capabilities.

This transition involves:

- Letting go of control and trusting others with responsibility
- Creating learning environments for others to grow in the gift
- Building opportunities for shadowing, delegation, and leadership stretch

- Recognising and affirming potential before it's fully polished

It's not about perfection — it's about preparation.

Your goal isn't to hold everything together on your own. Your goal is to build a team and legacy that can sustain the work and carry it further than you ever could.

Creating Space for Others to Rise

When the gift of administration is visible and celebrated, it attracts others. But in many churches, the gift is still hidden. Potential administrative leaders may never rise because they've never seen someone doing it boldly, joyfully, and spiritually.

You can change that.

Here's how:

Model the gift publicly: Let others see how Spirit-filled administration looks in action.

Invite others into the process: Don't just do the work — share your why and how.

Affirm the gift in others: Tell them what you see. Speak life over their ability to lead with structure, wisdom, and care.

Challenge assumptions: Help shift the narrative that administration is "just a support role."

You're not just preparing spreadsheets — you're preparing successors.

Laying the Groundwork for Chapter 18

In the next chapter, we'll explore what it means to develop administrative leaders — practically, spiritually, and strategically. We'll look at how to create pipelines, mentorship models, training programmes, and healthy team culture that elevates this gift across your church or organisation.

But before we get there, pause and ask yourself:

Am I building for today or for tomorrow?

What legacy am I creating for the next generation of administrators?

How can I steward my influence not only for efficiency — but for equipping?

The work you do now matters.

But the leaders you raise?

They will multiply that work into the future.

Final Thoughts

As we look ahead to the next phase of this journey, one thing is clear: the gift of administration must not only be practised — it must be passed on.

The future of healthy churches, effective ministries, and sustainable mission work depends on our willingness to multiply what we carry. We cannot afford to be the last stop in the line of Spirit-empowered administrators. We must be the link that prepares, equips, and releases the next.

Your calling is not just to build — it's to build others.

Your influence is not just in what you manage — it's in who you mentor.

And your legacy is not just in what you finish — it's in who you prepare to start.

As we move into Chapter 18, we'll step into the practical and spiritual work of developing administrative leaders — identifying them, training them, and creating a culture where the gift is recognised, nurtured, and released for the glory of God.

You've carried the gift well. Now it's time to prepare others to do the same.

18

Developing Administrative Leaders

Every administrator has the opportunity—and responsibility—to raise others up. Leadership development isn't just for pastors or preachers. Those with the gift of administration are called to equip others who can build, organise, and support ministry infrastructure. This is not only wise stewardship of the workload — it's Kingdom multiplication.

When administrators invest in new leaders, they protect the ministry from burnout, bottlenecks, and transition crises. Developing administrative leaders ensures sustainability and long-term health for the church. Without a leadership pipeline, churches become over-reliant on a few and vulnerable to disruption when transitions or emergencies occur. But when administrators are intentional about training others, they leave behind a legacy of excellence that outlives their position.

The Biblical Mandate for Multiplication

Paul wrote to Timothy, "The things you have heard me say in the presence of many witnesses entrust to reliable people who will also be qualified to teach others" (2 Timothy 2:2). This principle applies to administration too. What God has taught you to build, you must teach others to steward. It is a model of generational investment, one leader equipping the next with tools, mindset, and wisdom.

Moses applied this wisdom when Jethro advised him to appoint capable leaders to share the load (Exodus 18). Nehemiah trained and assigned crews to rebuild the wall. Jesus, the ultimate leader, trained twelve and released them to lead. The early church followed this pattern by appointing deacons in Acts 6 to manage daily distribution and support the apostles.

Multiplication is not optional — it is biblical. Developing others honours God's design for the Church and ensures that the mission continues with strength and order.

Steps to Developing New Administrative Leaders

1. Identify Potential Leaders

Look for people with natural organisational instincts, faithfulness in small things, teachability, and a servant heart. Don't overlook the quiet, behind-the-scenes contributors—they're often your best candidates. Look for those who ask good questions, anticipate needs, or offer help before being asked.

2. Model the Mission

People learn what administration looks like by watching you. Let them shadow your meetings, observe your planning process, and witness how you solve problems with wisdom and grace. Don't just show them what you do—explain why it matters and how it serves the bigger picture.

3. Document What You Do

Great administrators think in systems. Writing down policies, checklists, workflows, templates, and communication protocols makes it easier to train others—and creates long-term stability for your church. Think of your documentation as ministry inheritance.

4. Empower and Delegate

Don't wait until you're exhausted to ask for help. Delegate tasks with clear expectations and then step back to let people lead. Mistakes are part of learning. Provide feedback, but don't micromanage. Create a culture where learning is safe and progress is celebrated.

5. Celebrate and Affirm

Many people who serve administratively don't know they're operating in a spiritual gift. Call it out. Let them know their work is meaningful, anointed, and necessary for the Kingdom. Affirmation activates growth and builds confidence.

Creating a Development Pathway

If you want administrative leadership to grow in your church, create an intentional pathway. This could include:

A structured volunteer onboarding process

Leadership training workshops tailored to admin tasks

Regular review and mentoring meetings

Opportunities to lead projects with oversight

A discipleship-based leadership culture

Each step should build confidence, character, and competence. Use progression models (e.g., beginner, developing, advanced) to track and support their growth.

Real-Life Example: Emma's Journey

Emma started as a volunteer helping at the welcome desk. Her attention to detail and calm presence stood out. An administrator noticed her gifting, trained her in event planning, and eventually handed her the coordination of new guest follow-up. Today, Emma leads a team of volunteers and trains others in administrative ministry. She didn't come in asking to lead—but someone made space for her to grow. Emma's story illustrates how identifying and investing in one person can ripple into greater impact across the church.

Avoiding the Trap of Overdependence

One common mistake in churches is to place too much responsibility on one capable administrator. This leads to exhaustion and eventually limits ministry growth. A development mindset allows the administrator to:

Identify areas of replication

Empower multiple people to own key processes

Ensure continuity in case of absence or transition

Training others reduces bottlenecks and cultivates team resilience. It also makes room for diversity in administrative styles, innovation, and shared ownership.

Raising Leaders Across Generations

Don't just train those who are available now — invest in the next generation. Invite young people to participate. Show them that administration is not boring, but deeply spiritual and impactful. Host leadership clinics, create internship roles, or allow youth to assist with tech, planning, or data management. Pair emerging leaders with experienced mentors and celebrate their contributions.

Young leaders bring new ideas, digital fluency, and fresh perspective. When you invest in them early, they grow with the ministry. Make administration a part of your youth and young adult discipleship strategy.

Final Thoughts

Leadership is not about doing more. It's about multiplying impact. When you invest in others, you don't lose your role — you expand your reach.

Developing administrative leaders is an act of faith and legacy. It requires intentionality, patience, and prayer. Start now. Build slowly. Equip strategically. And watch how God grows His church through your obedience.

You are not just training helpers. You are releasing Kingdom builders. The systems you share today may serve thousands tomorrow. Steward your influence wisely, and trust that the seeds you plant in others will bear fruit for years to come.

The Administrator's Spiritual Life

Behind every effective administrator is a spiritual life that sustains the work. While the tasks may seem practical, the fuel must be deeply spiritual. No matter how well you plan, lead, or execute — if your soul is dry, your ministry will eventually feel heavy, joyless, or routine.

This chapter is an invitation to prioritise your inner world — not as an afterthought, but as your first ministry. Your spreadsheets matter. But so does your spirit. Without spiritual depth, your administrative work becomes empty activity. But when rooted in prayer, rest, and the Word, your leadership becomes worship.

The Need for Rhythm and Rest

In Genesis, God created for six days and rested on the seventh. That rhythm wasn't just for creation — it was for us. Sabbath is not a suggestion; it is a spiritual principle. Administrators, by nature, often feel responsible for keeping things moving — but God calls you to stop, rest, and trust Him to hold the world together.

Rest is where:

- Your creativity is renewed
- Your identity is recalibrated
- Your spirit hears what your schedule often drowns out

In a culture that celebrates hustle, administrators must become countercultural people of rest. Sabbath doesn't mean inactivity; it means intentional stillness. It's an act of trust that God can do more in your rest than you can do in your striving.

Establish rhythms of Sabbath. Prioritise sleep. Take days off. Say no when you need to. Build margin into your week. You are not a machine. You are a servant, and even servants need refreshment.

Prayer-Fuelled Planning

Too often, we plan and then pray. But administrators are called to reverse the order — to pray before we plan. Before every project, meeting, or major decision, bring it before God.

James 1:5 reminds us, "If any of you lacks wisdom, you should ask God." Prayer is not a pause in the process — it is the power behind it.

Create space in your schedule for:

- Praying over your weekly tasks
- Asking God for clarity in decision-making
- Surrendering outcomes to His will
- Listening for divine redirection

Prayer is not a delay — it is the strategy. It recentres the administrator's heart, reminds them of their Source, and shifts the weight of responsibility back to the One who truly leads.

Scripture as Your Compass

As administrators, it's easy to become consumed by policies and procedures. But the Word of God must remain your primary guide. Let it shape your priorities, your responses, and your mindset.

Here are a few anchor scriptures for administrators:

1 Corinthians 14:40 — "Let everything be done decently and in order."

Colossians 3:23 — "Whatever you do, work at it with all your heart, as working for the Lord."

Proverbs 16:3 — "Commit to the Lord whatever you do, and he will establish your plans."

Meditate on these often. Speak them over your work. Let them guard your heart from frustration, comparison, or burnout. Place them in your workspace as reminders that your work is worship.

Guarding Against Spiritual Drift

Ministry can be demanding. And ironically, those who serve the most can sometimes become spiritually dry. The very gift that helps others thrive can leave the administrator feeling empty if not replenished regularly.

Signs of spiritual drift include:

- Constant fatigue without renewal
- Growing cynicism toward leadership or the church
- Feeling disconnected during worship
- Doing ministry out of duty rather than joy

If you feel yourself drifting:

- Don't ignore the signs — respond with intention
- Talk to a spiritual mentor or pastor

- Spend time in worship with no agenda
- Return to the reason you said yes to this calling in the first place

God does not need your performance. He desires your presence. When your heart is aligned with His, everything else flows from that sacred connection.

Practical Disciplines for Spiritual Strength

Here are a few daily or weekly practices to anchor you spiritually:

- Begin your workday with prayer and reflection
- Keep a devotional or journal in your workspace
- Post a scripture at your desk or planning wall
- Create quiet time in your calendar before major meetings or planning sessions
- Fast occasionally to draw nearer to God
- Join a small group or accountability circle

Small disciplines build spiritual resilience. They keep you rooted when the workload is heavy and the days are full. Spiritual practices are not extra — they are essential.

Final Thoughts

Your spiritual life is not a bonus to your administrative ministry — it is the foundation of it. Without it, the work becomes heavy. With it, the work becomes holy.

THE GIFT OF ADMINISTRATION

Return often to the quiet place. Let God remind you who you are, why you serve, and how deeply He delights in you. Let His presence be your source of wisdom, peace, and joy.

You are not just an administrator — you are a worshipper, a servant, and a dearly loved child of God.

Everything you do flows from that truth.

Leading Through Transition and Crisis

Change is inevitable. Whether it's a pastoral transition, a sudden crisis, a building move, or a global pandemic, seasons of transition can either destabilise a church — or strengthen it. In these moments, administrators play a critical role in providing stability, continuity, and clarity.

This chapter explores how administrators can lead well through times of change, ensuring that the mission continues, people remain cared for, and teams stay aligned.

Understanding the Nature of Transition

Transitions often bring a mix of emotions:

- Uncertainty about the future
- Anxiety over changing roles
- Grief for what is ending
- Excitement for what's ahead

Administrators help manage these emotional undercurrents by creating structure in the storm. Their steadiness brings peace. Administrators have the unique ability to maintain order while helping others navigate disorientation. When others feel unsettled, the administrator's calm presence can become a grounding force for teams and congregations alike.

During seasons of uncertainty, people need both empathy and structure. The administrator offers both.

The Anchor of Communication

In a transition, communication is everything. Without it, rumours grow and trust breaks down. Administrators should:

Develop clear communication plans

Provide timely updates to staff, volunteers, and the congregation

Clarify what's changing — and what's staying the same

Offer FAQs or transition guides when appropriate

Remember, people feel safe when they're informed. Even if all the answers aren't available, consistent updates communicate care and intentionality. Silence breeds speculation, but clear communication builds trust.

Use a variety of channels: email, newsletters, announcements, team meetings, and one-to-ones. Set a rhythm of communication so people know when and how they will be updated.

Systems That Sustain

Strong administrative systems help churches weather storms. These include:

- Documented processes and procedures
- Up-to-date contact and volunteer databases

- Budget plans and financial continuity strategies
- Digital file storage and backups
- Emergency response protocols

When things are in order, ministries can continue operating — even during leadership change or crisis. A healthy system allows the work of the ministry to outlast any one individual. It also allows for new leaders to step into clarity, rather than chaos.

Supporting the Senior Leader

In a crisis or transition, senior leaders carry immense pressure. Administrators can serve them by:

- Protecting their schedule and energy
- Taking ownership of operational tasks
- Offering prayer, encouragement, and wise counsel
- Being a sounding board without becoming overwhelmed

Your support strengthens their leadership. Sometimes what a senior leader needs most is someone they can trust to keep things running while they focus on people and vision. Administrators often become the invisible lifeline behind visible leadership.

Even small things matter: anticipating needs, creating briefing documents, setting reminders, managing timelines. These practical efforts become spiritual service.

Leading with Sensitivity and Strength

During change, some team members will need reassurance. Others will resist. Administrators should lead with:

- Empathy for those grieving change

- Courage to address tension or confusion
- Wisdom to know when to act and when to wait
- Flexibility to adjust systems as the season unfolds

Don't be afraid to acknowledge what people are feeling — while pointing them to the bigger picture. Strength doesn't mean detachment. Sensitivity is a strength when balanced with clarity and resolve.

Create safe spaces for feedback and dialogue. Lead meetings with presence and compassion. Allow room for grief while fostering hope.

Case Study: Steadying the Ship

When Pastor Lorna stepped down after 20 years, the church faced anxiety and confusion. Services continued, but momentum slowed. The church administrator, Kim, worked with the board to create a clear interim plan. Weekly email updates, open staff meetings, and a 90-day action calendar brought reassurance. When the new pastor arrived, they stepped into a church that had remained healthy and united.

Kim's leadership was not dramatic, but it was decisive. She held the team steady, diffused tension, and maintained mission focus. Her work behind the scenes was instrumental in a peaceful handover.

God's Purpose in the Shift

Romans 8:28 reminds us that "in all things God works for the good of those who love him." Even in disruption, God is forming something new. He works through the endings to make way for new beginnings.

Administrators must stay spiritually anchored. Spend time in prayer. Ask God for discernment. Trust that He is not only the God of order — He's the God of new beginnings. Your systems are not just survival tools — they are vessels of grace.

Hold to the truth that God is not surprised by change. He has already gone before you, and He is equipping you to steward what comes next.

Final Thoughts

Crisis and change will test your systems, your leadership, and your spirit. But they are also opportunities to demonstrate faith, wisdom, and resilience.

As an administrator, you are not just reacting to change — you are stewarding transition. Let your leadership bring calm to chaos, vision to uncertainty, and hope to every hallway you serve in.

Because when you lead well in the storm, you help the church stand — and even thrive — in the shifting winds of change.

Leaving a Legacy

As administrators, we are called to build for the long term — to sow seeds that outlast our tenure, to create systems that serve future leaders, and to disciple others who will continue the work long after we're gone. This is the heart of legacy: building what lasts.

Legacy is not about being remembered. It's about leaving behind something that continues to serve, grow, and bless. In the Kingdom of God, legacy is less about name recognition and more about fruit that remains.

The Biblical Vision of Legacy

Proverbs 13:22 says, "A good person leaves an inheritance for their children's children." Though often read financially, this principle applies to leadership as well. God honours those who think generationally — those who prepare the way for others.

Throughout Scripture, we see the model:

- Moses prepared Joshua

- Elijah prepared Elisha
- Paul mentored Timothy
- Jesus discipled the twelve

Each passed on more than tasks — they passed on trust, wisdom, and vision. Their legacy wasn't only in what they accomplished, but in who they raised.

What Legacy Looks Like for Administrators

Leaving a legacy means:

- Documenting systems and practices clearly
- Mentoring and empowering new leaders
- Creating team cultures built on grace, excellence, and discipleship
- Establishing values that endure beyond a single leader's influence

The best systems are the ones that continue working even when you're no longer there. Your legacy is not what you do, but what continues because of what you built.

Legacy is about leadership that outlives you.

Creating Transferable Systems

One of the greatest gifts an administrator can leave is clarity. Ensure that your knowledge is not trapped in your head. Capture it in:

- Digital files and resource folders
- Operations manuals or ministry handbooks
- Planning templates and process guides

- Password logs and access protocols

This isn't just about organisation — it's about honouring the people who will carry the work forward. Transferable systems reduce stress, protect continuity, and honour the next generation.

Think ahead: If you had to step away tomorrow, could someone else pick up where you left off? Build in a way that says "yes."

Raising Up Your Successor

Legacy thrives when succession is intentional. Don't wait until you're stepping down to prepare someone else. Reproducing your role is not a threat — it's a sign of maturity.

- Identify someone with character and capacity
- Invite them into planning and decision-making
- Let them shadow and lead with increasing responsibility
- Share the "why" behind the "how"

You are not replacing yourself — you are multiplying your impact. A true leader prepares the next generation and celebrates their success.

Create leadership opportunities where others can learn, grow, and lead. The healthiest teams are the ones preparing for succession while things are going well.

Humility in the Process

Leaving a legacy also requires humility. Letting go of control. Trusting others to lead differently. Celebrating what God does through the next generation, even if it looks different than what you built.

John the Baptist said, "He must become greater; I must become less" (John 3:30). That's legacy in its purest form. It's not about holding on — it's about lifting others up.

As administrators, we must resist the urge to become territorial. Instead, we must become stewards who gladly pass on what was never ours to keep.

Final Thoughts

Your spreadsheets may not make headlines. Your planning meetings may not trend online. But the systems, teams, and culture you build today can impact generations.

Leave with intention. Build with eternity in mind. Let your legacy be a church that is stronger, healthier, and more equipped to fulfil its mission — because you were faithful with your part.

Legacy is not found in your name. It's found in what continues because of your faithfulness.

Write the vision. Train the team. Pass the baton.

Your greatest impact might not be what you accomplish — but what lives on after you.

Reframing Excellence – Doing Ministry Well

Churches are called to operate with excellence, not perfection. As administrators, part of your spiritual leadership is helping create a culture where excellence is the norm — not to impress people, but to honour God.

Excellence in ministry means:

- Preparing with intention
- Communicating with clarity
- Planning with margin
- Executing with consistency

It's the difference between winging it and stewarding it. Excellence reflects the character of God, who is not haphazard or disorganised.

Biblical Excellence

Consider the detail in God's instructions for the tabernacle (Exodus 25–31). Every measurement, material, and placement mattered. Not because God needed gold — but because He desired honour. Nehemiah didn't just rebuild a wall — he assigned families, secured tools, planned strategy, and completed the work in 52 days.

Excellence is spiritual. It communicates care, diligence, and devotion. It invites trust. And it multiplies impact.

Practical Excellence in Administration

Plan ahead — avoid last-minute panic

Use checklists and templates to standardise success

Create room for feedback and post-event reviews

Equip volunteers with clear instructions and tools

Schedule rest into the calendar

Excellence doesn't mean doing more — it means doing things well.

Overcoming the Fear of Not Being Perfect

Some administrators confuse excellence with perfectionism. But they're not the same. Perfectionism says, "I must perform flawlessly to be worthy." Excellence says, "I will do my best to honour God and serve others."

Perfectionism leads to:

- Paralysis before projects begin
- Over-control and micromanagement
- Harsh self-talk and burnout

Grace-based excellence leads to:

- Confidence to take risks
- Collaboration and delegation
- Joy in the process, not just the outcome

Let grace fuel your drive for excellence. God is honoured by your heart as much as your results.

Final Thoughts

In administration, how you do things matters. Excellence is not about applause — it's about obedience. It's about creating systems, experiences, and environments that reflect the goodness and order of God.

Commit to a higher standard — not for recognition, but for reverence. Because when we do our work well, we don't just make ministry smoother — we make the Gospel more visible.

Excellence isn't extra. It's essential.

Creating a Culture of Honour in Administration

Culture is not built in a day — it's built daily. One of the most powerful cultures an administrator can help cultivate is a culture of honour. Honour creates safety, inspires excellence, and reflects the heart of God. In a church context, honour becomes the soil where trust, growth, and unity thrive.

The Power of Honour

In a culture of honour, people:

- Are valued not just for what they do, but for who they are
- Receive correction with grace because trust has been built
- Are empowered to contribute without fear of failure

When honour is present, relationships flourish. Teams function with joy. People feel seen, heard, and safe. This kind of atmosphere doesn't just happen — it's cultivated by intentional leaders who choose humility, kindness, and integrity.

The Biblical Foundation of Honour

Romans 12:10 says, "Outdo one another in showing honour." Honour is not just politeness — it's a Kingdom principle. It reflects how God treats His children and how He desires us to treat one another.

David honoured Saul even when Saul tried to kill him. Jesus honoured the poor, the outcast, and the overlooked. Paul honoured women, youth, and co-labourers by name in his letters. Honour is how heaven operates. It must also be how we lead.

When administrators build with honour, they reflect the divine nature of their calling. Honour is not weakness — it is strength under submission.

What Honour Looks Like in Administration

- Publicly affirming volunteers and team members
- Privately correcting with love and clarity
- Giving credit where it's due
- Not overloading faithful people just because they're capable
- Learning to say "thank you" and "well done" consistently

As administrators, we often manage people's time, skills, and availability. But we are also stewarding their dignity. Honouring people in the small moments builds trust for the big ones.

When systems are run with honour, people feel protected rather than used. Honour shifts the culture from transactional to transformational.

Honour Heals What Hierarchy Hurts

Churches sometimes adopt corporate models that elevate hierarchy over humility. But the Body of Christ is not a corporate ladder — it's a family. Honour bridges the gap between titles and relationships.

Administrators can:

- Model honour in meetings by listening well
- Speak up when someone is being disrespected or overlooked
- Build policies that protect, not just control
- Help leaders consider how decisions affect people on the ground

Honour isn't just a value — it's a leadership tool. It strengthens unity, promotes health, and gives weight to your voice.

Building Honour into Systems

You don't need to wait for a meeting to speak honour. It can be embedded in your systems:

- Create feedback loops where every voice can be heard
- Use surveys and suggestion boxes with follow-up
- Schedule regular team check-ins for encouragement and evaluation
- Include testimonies and shout-outs in team communications

Systems don't have to be sterile. They can carry warmth, affirmation, and honour. A spreadsheet can reflect the heart of Christ when it's used to build people, not just plans.

Final Thoughts

Honour makes people want to stay. It makes teams feel like family. It builds bridges between departments and leaders. It cultivates trust, belonging, and joy.

As an administrator, you help set the tone. Lead with honour — and watch how it transforms the atmosphere, strengthens the team, and reflects the heart of Jesus in everything you do.

Choose honour daily. Not just with your words, but with your systems, your planning, and your leadership.

Because honour doesn't just bless people — it invites the presence of God.

Spiritual Discernment in Administrative Decision-Making

Administration is not just about strategy — it's about spiritual discernment. While systems and logic are critical, effective church administration also requires a sensitivity to the Holy Spirit. Administrators must learn to listen for God's direction and align plans with His timing and purpose.

Discernment is the ability to perceive what is right, timely, and aligned with God's will. It invites us to pause, pray, and seek divine insight before acting. It acknowledges that even the most efficient plan is empty if it isn't empowered by God's wisdom. Spiritual discernment is the difference between moving in human strength and moving under divine direction.

Why Discernment Matters in Administration

You may be tempted to rely on what worked before — or on what looks successful elsewhere. But every church is unique. Every season is different. What seems practical may not always be right.

Discernment protects the church from:

- Moving ahead of God
- Making decisions based on fear or pressure
- Adopting trends that don't suit the mission
- Prioritising speed over substance

Administrators need more than plans — they need prayerful perspective. When discernment is present, your decisions are not just efficient — they are prophetic. You begin to sense when to act, when to pause, and when to pivot. It allows for alignment between what is happening practically and what God is orchestrating spiritually.

Discernment also prevents burnout. When leaders rely solely on planning without spiritual guidance, the pressure to perform can become overwhelming. Discernment reminds us that the weight of the ministry is not on our shoulders alone — it's in God's hands.

Biblical Examples of Discernment

Joseph interpreted Pharaoh's dreams and prepared Egypt for famine with divine wisdom. His administrative excellence was empowered by prophetic insight. He not only interpreted the dream but executed a national survival plan with vision.

Daniel navigated complex government systems without compromising his convictions. He understood spiritual timing in a political world. Daniel's prayers, visions, and integrity set him apart as a leader who could be trusted by both God and kings.

Nehemiah sensed when to speak and when to wait, when to build and when to defend. His leadership flowed from prayer and discernment. His prayerful leadership enabled him to complete a massive rebuilding project amid opposition and discouragement.

Each of them administrated well because they listened to God first. Their systems were successful not just because of skill, but because of spiritual sensitivity. They teach us that strategy and discernment must walk hand-in-hand.

Practicing Spiritual Discernment

Pause and Pray: Don't rush major decisions. Create space to ask, "God, what do You want to do here?" Hold planning meetings that begin with stillness, not just strategy. This discipline cultivates spiritual attentiveness in your leadership.

Invite Counsel: Discernment often comes in community. Involve spiritual leaders, mentors, and trusted voices. Sometimes the insight you need is in someone else's perspective. Don't confuse solitude with isolation. God often speaks through godly counsel.

Check for Peace: Even in challenging decisions, the Holy Spirit often brings a sense of peace and confirmation. Don't override your inner checks for the sake of convenience. Pay attention to that sense of unease or peace — it is often God's guidance.

Search the Scriptures: God's Word will never contradict His Spirit. Use it to test and affirm your plans. Ask: Is this aligned with God's character and mission? Scripture is our compass, especially when emotions or pressures threaten to cloud our judgement.

Discern the Season: Not every good idea is for now. Timing is part of wisdom. Ecclesiastes 3:1 reminds us that "there is a time for everything." A discerning administrator recognises the difference between what is good and what is right for now.

Practice Listening: Discernment requires space to hear God. Make space in your personal and team rhythms for silence, reflection, and journaling. Create an environment where listening becomes part of the workflow.

Balancing Discernment and Delegation

Discernment does not mean becoming indecisive or overly spiritualising every detail. It means being open to the Spirit as you lead with structure. Invite God into your workflow — from the calendar to the boardroom.

You can:

- Listen for His prompting in leadership decisions
- Pause and pray before finalising major plans
- Ask for discernment in hiring, budgeting, and scheduling
- Train your team to recognise and respond to the Spirit too

Discernment sharpens your strategy. It helps you say "no" with peace and "yes" with purpose. It reduces regret and multiplies fruit. It enables wise delegation — knowing not only what to hand off, but to whom and when. This keeps teams healthy and decisions Spirit-led.

Discerning leaders don't need to control everything — they empower others with clarity and spiritual covering. Delegation becomes an act of trust, both in people and in God.

Developing Discernment Over Time

Discernment is not a gift only for the spiritually elite — it is available to all believers who seek it. Like any muscle, it grows with use.

Spend time daily in the Word and in prayer

Keep a journal of your decisions and their outcomes

Reflect on how God has led you in the past

Seek feedback from those you trust

Over time, you'll develop a greater sensitivity to God's voice and a deeper confidence in your choices.

Final Thoughts

The gift of administration is deeply spiritual when paired with discernment. You are not just leading logistics — you are stewarding the atmosphere, rhythm, and direction of God's people.

Ask often: "God, what are You doing here — and how can I join You?"

Let your plans be Spirit-led, your systems be prayer-born, and your leadership be shaped by the wisdom that only heaven can give.

Because administration isn't just about what works. It's about what God is blessing. Lead accordingly.

25

Ministering to Volunteers and Ministry Teams

Volunteers are the heartbeat of most churches. Without their service, many ministries simply wouldn't function. From welcoming teams and children's ministry workers to setup crews, intercessory teams, and worship assistants, the body of Christ relies heavily on the faithfulness of people who serve without financial compensation. Yet in the busyness of ministry life, it is easy for volunteers to feel burned out, under-appreciated, or directionless — especially when organisational systems are unclear or when leadership becomes overly task-focused.

This is where administrators play a vital and often unseen role. More than scheduling coordinators or logistics organisers, administrators are uniquely positioned to steward volunteers with care and to minister to them with love, grace, and wisdom. The way we lead, structure, and support volunteer teams can either build up or wear down the very people who are pouring themselves out for the work of the Kingdom.

The Heart of Volunteer Leadership

It's important to recognise that volunteers aren't just "free labour" or fill-ins when budget constraints prevent hiring staff. They are servants of God, often deeply committed to their church community, giving their time, energy, and hearts to the mission of Christ. Administrators who understand this don't lead from a place of control, but from compassion. Their approach is marked by:

Compassion over control – rather than simply delegating tasks or enforcing rules, they seek to understand the individual behind the role.

Encouragement over expectation – they speak life into volunteers, affirming their gifts, celebrating their efforts, and expressing gratitude regularly.

Support over supervision – their role isn't to micromanage, but to empower, troubleshoot, and make it easier for volunteers to succeed.

When administrators view volunteers as ministers rather than helpers, their entire leadership style changes. Volunteers are not secondary to paid staff — they are co-labourers in the harvest. They are worthy of honour, investment, and care.

Creating a Volunteer Culture of Joy and Ownership

A healthy volunteer culture doesn't just happen — it is cultivated intentionally. When volunteers feel purpose-driven, appreciated, and connected to the broader vision of the church, they serve with joy and enthusiasm. Administrators have the ability to help shape such a culture through thoughtful systems and spirit-led interactions.

A thriving volunteer culture is one where people:

> Know their purpose – they understand how their role contributes to the mission of the church.

Feel connected to the vision – they can articulate how their team fits into the church's overall direction.

Understand what's expected of them – clear communication and role descriptions eliminate confusion.

Receive appreciation regularly – both informal encouragement and formal recognition are essential.

Administrators can build this kind of culture through several practical avenues:

Clear onboarding and training – new volunteers should feel welcomed, informed, and prepared. An onboarding process with training manuals, mentoring, and Q&A sessions sets the tone for longevity and confidence.

Consistent scheduling and communication – using tools like church apps, WhatsApp groups, or shared calendars keeps everyone informed and helps prevent last-minute surprises. Clarity reduces stress.

Debriefs and development feedback – after major events or seasons, checking in with volunteers to gather feedback and offer constructive guidance communicates value and respect.

Celebrations and encouragement – whether it's a yearly volunteer appreciation dinner, handwritten thank-you notes, or spontaneous "we see you" shoutouts during team meetings, honouring your team refreshes the soul.

People serve with joy when they feel seen, heard, and celebrated.

Volunteer Burnout: How to Prevent It

Even the most passionate servant can burn out without the right structures of care and support. Burnout is more than just physical tiredness — it can be emotional exhaustion, spiritual fatigue, and a loss of joy in serving. Common signs include:

- Decreased enthusiasm or inconsistent attendance
- Irritability, frustration, or disengagement
- Withdrawal from communication or community
- Avoiding responsibility without explanation

Preventing burnout is a key responsibility of administrative leaders. Some practical strategies include:

Building margin into schedules – avoid overloading your most faithful volunteers by ensuring fair rotations and adequate rest periods.

Rotating responsibilities – allow volunteers to try different roles or take breaks after intense ministry seasons.

Respecting their time outside of church – avoid assuming 24/7 availability and encourage healthy boundaries.

Encouraging rest and Sabbath – promote rhythms of rest and remind volunteers that spiritual health matters more than performance.

It is not unspiritual to step back and recharge — in fact, it is necessary for longevity. Healthy volunteers lead healthy ministries, and healthy ministries are sustainable, joyful, and fruitful.

Empowering Team Leaders

While administrators often provide the structural foundation for ministry teams, it's essential that leadership is shared and multiplied. Rather than centralising control, administrators should empower team leaders — individuals who can carry vision, care for people, and manage their own groups effectively.

Empowered team leaders can:

Manage their own rotations and rosters – freeing up administrators from being the sole scheduler.

Encourage spiritual and personal development – helping their team members grow in faith and skill.

Resolve basic conflicts within their teams – rather than escalating every issue, trained leaders can navigate relational dynamics.

Provide feedback up the chain – offering insights and updates to administrators helps improve the overall system.

Training up leaders within teams is not a luxury — it's a necessity. It multiplies ministry effectiveness, prevents administrative bottlenecks, and cultivates future leaders within the church.

Provide these leaders with clear expectations, coaching, and encouragement, and you'll find that your ministry impact expands well beyond what any one administrator could manage alone.

Ministering Through Administration

Some people assume that administration is a "behind the scenes" task that's purely logistical. But in the Kingdom of God, everything we do — even spreadsheets and rotas — is a form of ministry when done with love and intention.

Every schedule, email, form, and planning meeting is an opportunity to express value and to care for people. Volunteer ministry thrives when:

Systems are servant-hearted, not task-driven – volunteers are not just names in a scheduling system; they are people with gifts and lives and needs.

People are prayed for, not just planned for – include prayer as part of your workflow. Pray over the schedule. Pray for wisdom in decision-making. Let volunteers know they are being lifted up.

The gospel is central to every ministry touchpoint – remind people why they're serving. Ministry isn't just to fill roles but to point others to Jesus. Every usher, every children's worker, every parking lot greeter is playing a part in the bigger gospel story.

Your role as an administrator is deeply pastoral, even if it looks practical.

Final Thoughts

Volunteers are not cogs in a machine — they are co-labourers in the harvest field. Administrators who lead with heart, vision, and honour create environments where people don't just serve — they thrive, grow, and stay.

When you minister to volunteers with intentionality, you don't just retain them — you release them into their calling. You help them discover joy in service, maturity in faith, and fruitfulness in ministry.

Remember: the best administrative systems are not simply efficient — they are life-giving. They support the work of the ministry, honour the people who carry it, and make room for the Holy Spirit to move freely through the gifts of every volunteer.

Let us never take for granted the sacred trust of those who serve alongside us. Let us lead with grace, serve with diligence, and minister with the heart of Christ.

Reimagining Church Operations for Future Growth

The Church is not a fixed institution — it is a living, breathing body, ever being shaped by the Holy Spirit, continually responding to cultural shifts, and always being called into greater maturity and transformation. As such, church operations must evolve alongside its mission. Administrators play a vital role in this movement. They are not merely caretakers of what has been but visionaries and architects of what could be. Their insight, discernment, and strategic acumen allow the Church to thrive not just today, but in the days to come.

This chapter explores how to transition church operations from maintenance to momentum, survival to scalability, and routine to innovation — all while preserving the spiritual essence and sacred purpose of the Church.

Evaluating What's Working (and What's Not)

Before embarking on change, the wise administrator pauses to evaluate. Innovation is not always about adding new things — often, it begins with pruning, clarifying, and re-aligning what already exists.

Begin by asking some foundational questions:

> Are our current systems and processes still serving the mission of the church?
>
> Do our teams understand their roles, timelines, and expectations clearly?
>
> Are we repeatedly fixing the same problems that better systems could solve?

A regular, intentional audit of ministry operations is a necessary rhythm. Administrators must be willing to assess for:

Bottlenecks in communication – Are key messages being missed? Are decisions slow because too many people are in the loop or the wrong ones are?

Gaps in team coverage – Are there areas of ministry that are suffering because no one has been assigned, trained, or equipped to lead?

Outdated or underused tools – Are we still using paper sign-up sheets when digital options could simplify the process? Are we paying for software that no one is using?

One of the most strategic things a church administrator can do is create space for honest evaluation — and to do so with humility, curiosity, and a growth mindset. This isn't about criticism, it's about clarity.

Embracing Innovation with Discernment

Innovation is a buzzword in many leadership spaces, but in the context of the Church, it must be handled with spiritual maturity and discernment. Being future-minded doesn't mean jumping on every trend or rushing to adopt the latest technology. It means making strategic decisions with a Kingdom mindset, rooted in prayer, community input, and wise counsel.

Ask yourself:

What tools, platforms, or processes could genuinely increase our impact?

How can we simplify our workflows without sacrificing quality or pastoral care?

What's one inefficient system we could improve this quarter?

Not every change has to be revolutionary. Start small. Introduce pilot programmes or beta testing phases before rolling out new tools or methods across the entire church. This gives people time to adjust, provides valuable feedback, and allows for course correction.

Moreover, honour what has come before. Not all "old" systems are broken — many are simply awaiting a refresh or a new champion. Honour the traditions and sacrifices of past leaders while helping the church embrace new tools and ideas that position it to better serve the next generation.

Discernment keeps innovation anchored in truth and humility. It ensures that change serves the mission — not ego or convenience.

Designing for Growth and Scale

Churches that desire to grow must design systems that scale. You cannot pour new wine into old wineskins. If we believe God will bring increase — whether in people, resources, or influence — we must create operational structures that can sustain that growth.

Some practical ways to do this include:

Documenting processes – Instead of relying on one person's memory or style, create process guides that anyone can follow. This empowers new leaders and guards against burnout or turnover causing disruption.

Cross-training teams – Avoid single-person dependency by equipping multiple people to perform key roles. When team members know how to support one another, the ministry becomes more resilient.

Streamlining communication – Use digital platforms like Slack, Planning Centre, or Microsoft Teams to reduce communication confusion. Keep messages clear, centralised, and consistent.

Planning capacity for growth – Is your physical space adaptable for future growth? Do your budgets have room to flex? Is there a leadership pipeline in place to raise up new leaders as the ministry expands?

Growth requires intentional preparation. The question isn't just, "Can we handle where we are now?" but, "If God sends more — more people, more needs, more vision — are we ready to steward it well?"

From Crisis Mode to Strategic Planning

Too many churches operate in reactive mode — always responding to the latest emergency, last-minute need, or Sunday morning scramble. While occasional crises are inevitable, living in a constant state of urgency is unsustainable and unhealthy.

Administrators can help churches shift from reaction to proaction by introducing rhythms of strategic planning:

Annual Planning Calendars – Map out the year with key dates, events, sermon series, team trainings, and major ministry initiatives. This gives everyone visibility and time to prepare.

Quarterly Ministry Reviews – Meet with each department or team every few months to evaluate what's working, what needs support, and what goals they want to pursue next.

Long-Term Forecasting – Consider the needs of your building, budget, and staffing five to ten years from now. Start planning now for renovations, new hires, or debt retirement.

Scenario Planning – Think through "what if" situations. What if attendance doubles? What if we lose a key staff member? What if giving decreases by 20%? These exercises aren't fear-driven — they're wisdom-led.

The Church's future isn't something to dread. It's a field waiting to be sown into. Strategic planning makes sure that when the harvest comes, the storehouses are ready.

The Spiritual Integrity of Operational Growth

In all the talk of systems, scaling, and strategy, we must never forget the spiritual foundation of church operations. This isn't business — it's Kingdom work. The Spirit of God should be just as present in our spreadsheets as He is in our sermons. The way we handle logistics is a form of worship, a ministry of stewardship and care.

Growth must not come at the expense of spiritual depth. Innovation must not overtake intimacy with God. Let every plan be held with open hands and bathed in prayer. Let every meeting begin with Scripture or devotion. Let every system be evaluated not just for efficiency, but for alignment with biblical values and pastoral sensitivity.

As administrators, we model what it means to serve the Church not only with excellence but with reverence. We are building something holy — not just operational, but eternal.

Final Thoughts

The Church of tomorrow will be shaped by the systems we build today. Administrators are not just behind-the-scenes workers; they are spiritual architects and visionary leaders. Through faithful stewardship, discerning innovation, and strategic foresight, administrators help the Church move forward with grace and strength.

You are not simply managing tasks. You are designing a future. One where the Church is agile in its structure, anointed in its purpose, and ready to disciple the next generation with excellence and joy.

So reimagine boldly. Build faithfully. Let every process be soaked in prayer, every plan rooted in purpose, and every change led by the Spirit. The Church is moving forward — and your leadership is paving the way.

The Role of the Administrator in Church Planting

Church planting is one of the most exciting and demanding expressions of ministry. It is a bold declaration of faith — a willingness to step into the unknown, believing that God is birthing something new. New churches are often characterised by vibrant vision, passionate teams, and deep reliance on the Holy Spirit. But alongside all that passion lies a critical need: structure. Without it, even the most Spirit-led church plants can stumble into burnout, financial strain, or administrative disarray.

This is where administrators shine.

While church planters are often the prophetic voice and visionary leaders, administrators are the architects who construct the practical framework to sustain the vision. They bring order to chaos, clarity to complexity, and stewardship to every seed of growth. Church planting is not just a spiritual exercise — it's a logistical one too. And administrators ensure that what is planted has the foundation to flourish.

Starting with Strategy

Church plants usually begin with three powerful ingredients: passion, people, and prayer. These are non-negotiables — spiritual vitality must always be the centre of the new work. However, very quickly, the need for strategy emerges. Without basic infrastructure, the church plant can become overwhelmed by its own enthusiasm.

An administrator ensures that strong foundations are laid early — not just spiritually, but structurally. This includes:

Budgeting and basic accounting – Even before a formal launch, church plants need a financial plan. How will donations be tracked? What platform will be used for giving? What are the expected startup costs, and how will they be met? A clear budget sets boundaries and ensures transparency.

Volunteer coordination systems – In the beginning, everyone wears multiple hats. But even small teams need clarity around who is doing what, when, and how. Administrators can help create schedules, build rotas, and track team commitments to avoid duplication or confusion.

Communication platforms – How will the team stay connected? Whether through group chats, email lists, shared calendars, or project management tools, communication systems are essential from day one. They help ensure that the right information reaches the right people at the right time.

Legal and policy documents – This includes church incorporation, insurance, safeguarding policies, and any local regulations that must be adhered to. While planters are often focused on vision casting and people gathering, administrators handle the behind-the-scenes details that protect and legitimise the church's operations.

Strategy is not a distraction from the mission — it is what allows the mission to grow with integrity.

THE GIFT OF ADMINISTRATION

Building with Agility

Church plants are inherently dynamic. Things change fast. Plans shift. New people arrive. Venues become unavailable. Leaders get stretched. Administrators must embrace this fluidity with grace and wisdom.

Agility is the administrator's superpower. In the early phases, administrators are required to:

Adapt to rapid growth – When a small group suddenly becomes a congregation, systems must scale quickly. What worked for 10 people may no longer work for 50 or 100.

Create evolving systems – Don't over-build too early. Instead, create frameworks that can grow and change over time. For example, using a simple Google Sheet might suffice for early rotas, but as the church grows, a more robust volunteer management system may be necessary.

Keep it lean – Avoid the temptation to overcomplicate. Keep policies simple, processes clear, and tools easy to use. Remember, simplicity does not mean disorder. It means structure that serves the mission, not structure that stifles it.

In the early stages, the administrator is often a jack-of-all-trades — helping with logistics, Sunday setup, data tracking, kids' check-in, and even tech support. The ability to stay flexible while maintaining excellence is what makes an administrator indispensable during a plant's fragile beginnings.

Managing Momentum

Once the church plant gains traction and begins to grow, momentum becomes a powerful but delicate force. Growth brings energy — but it also brings complexity. If not managed well, it can lead to team fatigue, communication breakdown, and misaligned priorities.

Administrators help manage this momentum by:

Creating sustainable rhythms – Weekly services, midweek meetings, outreach events, and pastoral care all need to be balanced. Administrators help pace the ministry so that leaders and volunteers don't burn out.

Scaling systems – As attendance increases, so must the capacity of your systems. This includes check-in procedures, welcome teams, children's ministry protocols, and data collection. Growth should not outpace operational readiness.

Distributing the load – Founding pastors often carry a heavy burden. Administrators can help alleviate this by developing teams, assigning responsibilities, and ensuring that no one person becomes a bottleneck for the church's effectiveness.

Momentum doesn't need to be chaotic. When stewarded well, it becomes a launching pad for long-term impact.

Championing the Vision

Great administrators are not just implementers — they are culture carriers and vision champions. They help guard the heart of the ministry while enabling its hands and feet to function effectively.

Some key ways administrators champion the vision include:

Speaking life into the leadership – Church planting can be isolating. Planters need encouragement, perspective, and sometimes just someone to remind them they're not alone. A supportive administrator becomes a safe sounding board and trusted advisor.

Guarding against mission drift – As new opportunities arise, it's easy for church plants to lose focus. Administrators help keep decisions aligned with the original mission and values by asking: Does this serve the vision? Is this the right time?

Maintaining clarity – Administrators help clarify roles, priorities, and boundaries. In a season where "everyone does everything," they create order out of chaos. They ensure that vision doesn't get diluted by disorganisation.

Ultimately, administrators embody the "how" behind the "why." They give vision feet.

Final Thoughts

Church planters are often seen as trailblazers — bold, passionate, and ready to pioneer. But no pioneer succeeds alone. When planters partner with administrators early in the journey, they don't just build faster — they build stronger, deeper, and healthier.

Administrators are essential from day one. Not as an afterthought, but as co-builders of the house of God.

If you are called to plant a church, prayerfully consider inviting an administrative leader into your core team from the start. Their presence will provide stability, foresight, and the kind of structure that allows vision to take root and bear fruit.

And if you are an administrator, know this: your calling is vital. Church planting needs your gifts — not eventually, but immediately. You are not just launching a service or coordinating logistics. You are helping to build a dwelling place for the presence of God, a beacon of hope in the community, and a new expression of the Kingdom.

Every house needs a solid structure to last. You are laying the bricks, one system, one strategy, one Spirit-led decision at a time. And because of your faithfulness, the Church will not just be planted — it will grow, flourish, and endure.

How to Build a Healthy Administrative Team

Great administration rarely happens in isolation. Behind every smoothly functioning church are faithful, capable, and often unseen individuals who support, organise, plan, and execute the operations that make ministry possible. Whether paid staff or dedicated volunteers, these teams ensure that the vision of the church is not only proclaimed but practically implemented.

But healthy administrative teams don't just materialise. They are prayerfully formed, intentionally developed, and lovingly led. A thriving team doesn't merely get things done — it becomes a reflection of Christ's body working together in unity and purpose.

This chapter explores how to build, grow, and sustain an administrative team that is not only effective, but spiritually vibrant and relationally healthy.

THE GIFT OF ADMINISTRATION

Start with the Right People

Every strong team starts with individuals who are not just willing, but well-suited to the work. While enthusiasm is important, so is alignment. Administrative work often involves repetitive tasks, attention to detail, and patient problem-solving — qualities that don't always appeal to everyone. It's essential to discern gifting as well as willingness.

Look for individuals who are:

Detail-oriented and dependable – People who enjoy organising, checking for errors, and following through on tasks.

Spiritually mature and humble – Administrative decisions affect the whole church. You need team members who are spiritually grounded, prayerful, and not motivated by ego.

Comfortable working behind the scenes – Not everyone needs a platform to make an impact. Some of the most powerful ministry happens off-stage.

Team players who value collaboration – Administration isn't a solo act. Look for those who work well with others and contribute to a team dynamic.

It's tempting to recruit based on availability alone, but that can lead to frustration for both the team and the individual. Don't just invite people who "have time." Seek those who understand the value of administrative ministry and carry the heart of your church's mission. Pray before you recruit. Look for character over charisma, faithfulness over flair.

Define Clear Roles

One of the quickest ways to frustrate an administrative team is through role ambiguity. Confusion breeds tension. Without clearly defined roles, tasks fall through the cracks, expectations go unmet, and miscommunication becomes the norm.

Take time to define and communicate each team member's responsibilities. Some important questions to ask include:

- Who is responsible for scheduling events and volunteers?
- Who handles financial tracking or reporting?
- Who manages digital tools or maintains databases?
- Who liaises with ministry leaders to gather information or distribute resources?

Don't assume people will "just figure it out." Put it in writing. Create a shared document or team manual that outlines roles and duties. Clarify lines of accountability — not as a way to control, but to empower.

Also, revisit roles regularly. As ministries grow and evolve, responsibilities may need to shift. Some tasks may become too burdensome for one person, or someone may discover a gift for an area they didn't expect. Flexibility with clarity is key.

Train and Equip Continuously

Even the most gifted volunteers need training. Enthusiasm without knowledge can lead to mistakes. Confidence grows when people are given tools, context, and ongoing support.

Key areas of training include:

- Orientation for new members – Introduce them to your systems, your vision, and your expectations. Don't just throw them in the deep end.
- Cross-training – This builds resilience. If one team member is absent, others can step in and cover without disruption.
- Ongoing development – Offer occasional refreshers, skill-building sessions, or leadership development opportunities. Keep the team learning.

It's also helpful to provide:

- Manuals or how-to guides
- Cheat sheets for commonly used tools
- Login access to scheduling or project platforms
- Lists of contacts for support and communication

Don't leave your team guessing. When you invest in their growth, you're not just building skill — you're communicating value.

Communicate Regularly and Clearly

Communication is the glue of any team. Without it, even the best systems can unravel. In administrative ministry, where so many details are in motion, clear and consistent communication is non-negotiable.

Here are some ways to keep your team connected:

Weekly or bi-weekly check-ins – Whether by video, phone, or in-person, regular rhythm builds accountability and gives space to ask questions.

Shared calendars or project trackers – Tools like Google Calendar, Trello, or Asana can help visualise deadlines and responsibilities.

Group chats or message boards – Platforms like WhatsApp, Slack, or Microsoft Teams create space for quick updates and encouragement.

Importantly, don't just communicate tasks. Communicate vision. Remind the team why their work matters. Celebrate wins. Share testimonies. Include prayer points or spiritual reflections. Keep your administrative meetings spiritually nourishing.

When people feel informed and inspired, they serve with clarity and joy.

Cultivate Unity and Care

Healthy teams are more than productive — they are relationally rooted. People are not machines. If the culture of your team is cold, transactional, or task-focused, it will lead to burnout and disengagement.

Create a culture where team members feel cared for, connected, and safe. Here are a few practices that help:

Start meetings with prayer – Not just out of routine, but as a sacred reminder that what you're doing is ministry.

Share personal updates – Take time to check in on each other's lives. Celebrate birthdays, acknowledge struggles, and build real relationships.

Recognise milestones and answered prayers – Celebrate moments like a major event going smoothly, a team member reaching a personal goal, or a breakthrough in a challenging system.

Encourage appreciation – Make it normal to say thank you, honour one another, and point out what's going well.

Teams that pray together, grow together. When people feel seen and valued beyond their output, they become more engaged, loyal, and joyful in their service.

Evaluate and Adjust

No system is perfect. No team remains static. Healthy administrative teams are willing to reflect, receive feedback, and make necessary adjustments.

Set regular times to evaluate:

What's working well?

What needs improvement?

Are there tools or systems that are no longer serving us?

Is anyone feeling overwhelmed or under-utilised?

Create a safe space for feedback — one where honesty is welcomed and defensiveness is left at the door. This isn't about perfection. It's about growth. Encourage innovation. Ask team members to suggest better ways of doing things. When people are empowered to speak into the process, they take more ownership of the outcome.

Healthy teams evolve over time — and that's a good thing.

Final Thoughts

A strong administrative team doesn't just support the church — it strengthens it. When people are serving in their strengths, clearly equipped, relationally connected, and united in vision, everything flows more smoothly. Ministry leaders can dream bigger. Congregants experience greater hospitality and care. The whole church becomes more agile and responsive to God's leading.

You're not just building a team — you're building trust, culture, and capacity. The health of your administrative team affects the health of the wider church. Invest well in your people. Equip them faithfully. Celebrate them regularly.

And remember: every form, rota, spreadsheet, and calendar you steward is not just an administrative task — it is a sacred contribution to the Kingdom of God.

Administrative Wisdom for Multicultural Churches

We live in a globalised world where the Church is increasingly becoming a reflection of the nations — diverse in ethnicity, language, customs, and culture. In many churches today, it's not uncommon to find congregants who hail from a dozen different countries, each carrying unique stories, traditions, and expressions of worship. While this diversity brings depth, beauty, and a fuller representation of the Kingdom of God, it also brings complexity.

Administrators, often working behind the scenes, are uniquely positioned to help navigate this complexity. They build the systems, plan the gatherings, coordinate the teams, and communicate across the congregation. Their choices — sometimes seemingly small — can determine whether a church environment feels inclusive or exclusive, welcoming or awkward, honouring or neglectful.

This chapter explores how administrative leadership can reflect the richness of the Body of Christ by fostering belonging, creating inclusive processes, and cultivating a culture of unity in diversity.

Understanding the Dynamics of Diversity

Multicultural churches are enriched by the presence of different languages, worship styles, family structures, learning preferences, leadership expectations, and communication styles. Each culture brings gifts, perspectives, and strengths to the table. But these gifts also come with challenges that, if not acknowledged, can lead to misunderstanding, division, or marginalisation.

Administrators must become students of these dynamics. It starts with recognising:

> Culture shapes expectations – For example, in some cultures, punctuality is non-negotiable; in others, flexibility is the norm. In some, leadership is hierarchical; in others, it's relational and communal.
>
> Language affects clarity – English may be spoken by many, but not always as a first language. Idioms, slang, and fast-paced delivery can unintentionally exclude or confuse.
>
> Norms are not universal – What is considered polite, sacred, or professional varies. Seating arrangements, order of service, and even food choices can carry different meanings in different cultures.

Administrators who operate with this awareness create systems that don't just function — they flourish across cultural lines.

Leading with Cultural Intelligence

Cultural Intelligence (CQ) is the ability to relate and work effectively across cultures. For administrators, CQ is not just a desirable quality — it is essential. Church systems are not neutral; they are shaped by the people who design them. When administrators bring cultural intelligence to their leadership, they create space for more people to feel seen, heard, and honoured.

The four components of CQ are:

Awareness – Know your own cultural lens. What assumptions do you carry? How might your own background be shaping the way you plan or communicate?

Knowledge – Take time to learn about the cultures represented in your church. Ask questions. Listen to stories. Attend cultural events. Understanding people's lived experiences strengthens community bonds.

Strategy – Plan with intentionality. Think through how systems, events, or messages will land with people from different backgrounds. What needs to be explained? What should be translated or adjusted?

Action – Be willing to adapt without losing sight of the mission. Flex where appropriate. Hold to core values, but with sensitivity and love.

Administrators who lead with CQ are not just efficient — they're transformational. They build systems that reflect the inclusivity of the gospel.

Inclusive Communication

Communication is a cornerstone of church administration, and inclusive communication is key to making a multicultural congregation feel truly unified.

Many churches unintentionally use "insider" language — acronyms, denominational jargon, or culturally-specific phrases — that confuse or exclude those who are new or from different backgrounds. Even things like bulletin announcements, signage, or stage directions can carry subtle cultural codes.

Administrators can help shift this by:

Offering multilingual resources – Translate key information into the primary languages spoken in your congregation. This could include bulletins, website content, welcome packets, and important signage.

Using inclusive visuals – Ensure that promotional materials, social media posts, and website photos reflect the cultural makeup of your church. Representation builds trust and communicates "you belong here."

Training welcome teams and volunteers – Teach those on the frontlines how to greet, assist, and connect with people from all backgrounds with grace, curiosity, and kindness.

Being mindful of tone – Whether in emails, WhatsApp groups, or public announcements, choose language that's clear, gracious, and accessible. Avoid sarcasm, assumptions, or cultural shorthand that may not translate.

When communication is handled with inclusivity and humility, it becomes a bridge rather than a barrier.

Programming with Inclusion in Mind

Inclusivity must be reflected not just in who is welcomed, but in how the church operates — especially in event planning and programming. From the moment people arrive to the final benediction, the way events are structured says a great deal about who is being considered.

Administrators can lead the way by:

Including diverse cultural elements – Incorporate food, music, and traditions that reflect the cultures within your congregation. During church picnics, Christmas parties, or shared meals, invite people to bring dishes from their heritage.

Scheduling with cultural awareness – Take into account major cultural or religious holidays from the communities you serve. Avoid scheduling leadership events during cultural festivals or family celebration days if possible.

Diverse representation on stage and behind the scenes – Whether it's through MCs, prayer leaders, worship teams, or leadership panels, include people from different backgrounds. Representation fosters belonging and breaks unspoken hierarchies.

Valuing cultural expressions of worship – Some cultures are expressive and demonstrative; others are reflective and quiet. Make room for both. Administrators can encourage a service structure that embraces variety rather than enforcing uniformity.

Inclusion isn't about tokenism or political correctness — it's about hospitality. It's about creating space where everyone's identity is acknowledged and honoured.

Building a Culture of Belonging

More than just strategy, administrators carry a heart posture that communicates belonging. This can be demonstrated through:

Listening sessions – Host feedback forums where people from different cultures can share their experiences and offer input on church systems and practices.

Cultural liaisons – Appoint cultural connectors or advocates who help bridge gaps and raise awareness within leadership teams.

Celebrating diversity as a strength – Make it part of your language, your values, and your vision casting. The multicultural nature of the church isn't a challenge to be managed — it's a gift to be celebrated.

A culture of belonging is not built overnight. It's the fruit of consistent, prayerful effort to live out the gospel's radical welcome.

Final Thoughts

Administrators in multicultural churches have a sacred task: to build systems that whisper "you belong" even before a word is spoken. Through intentional leadership, inclusive planning, and humble cultural engagement, they play a powerful role in creating environments where every tribe, tongue, and nation can flourish together.

You don't just organise people. You honour them. You reflect the multifaceted beauty of the Body of Christ. You make the invisible visible. And in doing so, you help build a church that feels like home — for everyone.

The Church is not meant to be monochrome or monolithic. It is a mosaic — made vibrant by difference and held together by love. Your administrative leadership is the frame that holds that mosaic in place.

Rejoice in the diversity around you. Lead with curiosity. Communicate with care. And always, always build with the Kingdom in mind.

30

Digital Tools and Systems for Modern Church Administration

We are living in the digital age — a time when technology is rapidly shaping the way we work, communicate, and connect. The Church is not exempt from this shift. From how we manage Sunday volunteers to how people give, engage, and grow in discipleship, digital tools are now central to church life. Yet, while there are more tools available than ever before, wisdom in how we use them is what separates a church that is digitally cluttered from one that is digitally equipped.

Modern church administrators are not just managing files and scheduling meetings — they are curating digital ecosystems that support community, discipleship, and mission. This chapter is a practical guide for navigating that digital landscape with discernment, stewardship, and Spirit-led strategy.

Why Digital Stewardship Matters

Digital stewardship is more than convenience — it's about building systems that serve people. Whether a newcomer is trying to sign up for a welcome lunch, a parent is registering their child for youth ministry, or a volunteer is checking their schedule for Sunday service, digital systems directly impact their experience.

Digital tools affect how people:

- Sign up for ministries, events, or small groups
- Give and tithe, whether through mobile apps, websites, or kiosks
- Communicate with leaders, teams, and the wider church
- Access teaching materials, resources, and discipleship content
- Submit forms, prayer requests, or feedback

When these systems are clunky, confusing, or outdated, they cause frustration. When they are thoughtfully implemented, they facilitate connection, remove barriers to engagement, and help people feel valued.

A wise administrator sees technology not as a trend to follow, but as a tool to steward.

Core Tools Every Church Should Consider

While no two churches are identical, there are core categories of tools that most churches benefit from using. The key is to select tools that are scalable, user-friendly, and integrated into your ministry flow.

1. Church Management Software (ChMS)

Examples: Planning Centre, Breeze, Elvanto, Realm

These platforms serve as the digital "hub" for your church's operational life. Features often include:

- Attendance tracking
- Volunteer scheduling and rostering
- Giving records and donation tracking
- Pastoral care notes
- Group management (e.g. small groups, teams)

A good ChMS helps you keep your church family organised while also offering useful insights that aid in shepherding and strategic planning.

2. Communication Tools

Examples: Mailchimp, WhatsApp, Slack, Text-in-Church

Communication tools help maintain clear, timely, and consistent messages across your community. Some tools are best for:

- Mass communication (e.g. weekly emails, announcements)
- Team coordination (e.g. Slack or WhatsApp for quick updates)
- Visitor follow-up (e.g. automated text flows for first-time guests)

Pick tools that meet your audience where they are — some congregations are email-driven, others live in WhatsApp. Know your people.

3. Scheduling and Planning Tools

Examples: Google Calendar, Notion, Asana, Trello

Church life involves multiple moving pieces — events, meetings, rehearsals, prayer nights, and more. These tools help:

- Plan and delegate tasks
- Track deadlines
- Assign responsibilities

- Coordinate across departments

Asana or Trello is excellent for project planning, while Google Calendar provides shared scheduling visibility for teams.

4. Financial Systems

Examples: QuickBooks, Tithe.ly, Givelify, PayPal

Church finances must be managed with excellence and transparency. A robust digital giving platform should:

- Offer multiple giving options (web, app, recurring gifts)
- Integrate with your ChMS or accounting tools
- Provide clear reports for stewardship and legal compliance

Pair these platforms with financial software to manage budgets, expenses, and reporting.

5. File Sharing and Collaboration

Examples: Google Drive, Dropbox, Microsoft 365

With multiple leaders working on documents, plans, and resources, file sharing tools provide:

- Centralised storage of policies, sermons, and rotas
- Version control and document sharing
- Easy access across devices and locations

Use structured folders and clear naming conventions to stay organised and avoid "digital sprawl."

Best Practices for Implementation

Introducing new technology can be overwhelming. Without the right foundation, tools become underused or abandoned. Here are some best practices to implement digital tools successfully:

Start Simple

Don't attempt to launch five tools at once. Begin with your biggest pain point. Is volunteer scheduling a headache? Start with Planning Centre. Is communication chaotic? Try Slack or a WhatsApp group.

Master one tool, then add another.

Train Well

Equip your team. Don't assume digital fluency. Offer short training sessions, create simple how-to videos or PDFs, and be available for follow-up support.

People need to feel confident, not confused.

Integrate Wisely

Choose tools that integrate with one another. For example, a sign-up form on your website should feed directly into your ChMS, not require manual entry.

Integration saves time, reduces error, and increases adoption.

Review Regularly

Technology changes fast. Evaluate your digital systems every 6–12 months. Ask:

What are we using regularly?

What's no longer serving us?

Are there cheaper or better options available?

Regular reviews prevent tool fatigue and keep your systems sharp.

Protecting Data and Privacy

Churches handle sensitive information — giving records, prayer requests, children's details, volunteer applications. Administrators are stewards of this data and must ensure that proper protections are in place.

Some key safeguards include:

Adhering to data regulations – For example, GDPR in the UK/EU. Know what laws apply to your context.

Using strong passwords and multi-factor authentication – Especially for access to financial records or pastoral notes.

Limiting data access – Not every team member needs access to everything. Assign permissions based on role and necessity.

Communicating policies – Let your congregation know how their data is used, stored, and protected.

Digital trust is just as spiritual as it is practical. When people know their information is safe, they're more likely to engage.

Final Thoughts

Digital tools are not a replacement for prayer, wisdom, or relational ministry. They are a support — a scaffolding that allows the Church to function more freely, communicate more clearly, and serve more effectively.

CALLED TO ORGANISE. ANOINTED TO SERVE.

Administrators have the sacred task of building systems that reflect the values of the Kingdom: order, excellence, transparency, and care. As the digital world continues to evolve, the Church doesn't need to copy the world — it needs to lead with discernment.

Your role is not to chase every new app or trend, but to discern: What helps us serve people better? What enhances our mission? What tools free us to focus more on Jesus and less on admin overwhelm?

Let your systems serve your mission — not the other way around.

Measuring Impact and Evaluating Ministry Health

Effective administration is not merely about keeping things running — it's about why and how things are running. It's about ensuring that activity is aligned with purpose and that every resource, programme, and initiative is bearing fruit. In the Church, we are not just called to be busy — we are called to be fruitful. Our faithfulness must be coupled with stewardship, and stewardship involves evaluation.

Administrators are in a powerful position to help ministry leaders pause, reflect, assess, and adjust. When done with care and clarity, evaluation strengthens ministry health, encourages innovation, and deepens impact. It gives leaders the insight they need to make better decisions and helps volunteers see that their efforts are part of something meaningful.

This chapter explores how administrators can help foster a culture of review, utilise both data and stories to measure impact, and keep ministries aligned with the broader vision of the church.

Why Evaluation Matters

In the absence of evaluation, ministry efforts can drift into autopilot. Programmes may continue simply because "we've always done it this way." Events may be repeated year after year without considering whether they are still serving their intended purpose. Leaders may become discouraged because they can't see measurable results, and volunteers may begin to wonder if their efforts really matter.

Without evaluation:

Ministries may lose relevance – failing to adapt to the needs of the congregation or community.

Success becomes subjective – what one person sees as a "great turnout" another may see as a lack of engagement.

Volunteers may feel undervalued – when no one pauses to reflect on their efforts or to recognise their impact.

When administrators introduce regular, healthy review processes, they provide the Church with a gift: the ability to grow with intentionality.

Evaluating ministry health supports:

- Alignment with the church's mission and values
- Wise stewardship of time, finances, energy, and people
- Celebration of progress, even when it's incremental
- Insight into challenges, allowing for timely adjustments
- Stronger planning for future initiatives

Evaluation is not about judgment — it's about growth. It helps ensure that we are not just doing the right things, but doing the things right.

What to Measure

Measuring impact doesn't always mean counting numbers — though numbers can be helpful. In fact, both quantitative (data) and qualitative (stories and experiences) evaluation have a role in understanding ministry health.

Each church will measure different things depending on its size, context, and vision. However, some useful areas to consider include:

1. Attendance and Engagement Patterns

Are people showing up?

Are they returning and getting more involved?

Is there a trend in growth or decline in specific services or groups?

2. Volunteer Involvement and Retention

How many people are serving?

Are new volunteers being recruited and trained regularly?

Are long-time volunteers burning out or thriving?

3. Financial Health

Are giving levels consistent, increasing, or declining?

Are giving platforms easy to use and clearly communicated?

Is the church operating within its budget and stewarding funds well?

4. Discipleship Progression

How many people are involved in small groups or discipleship courses?

Are people being baptised, growing in their faith, or serving in new ways?

Are there stories of transformation or spiritual breakthrough?

5. Outreach and Community Impact

How many people are being served through outreach efforts?

Are follow-up systems in place for those who visit or receive ministry?

Are partnerships with local organisations bearing fruit?

Measuring these indicators helps determine where to invest more energy, where to refine processes, and where to celebrate growth.

Tools for Evaluation

The good news is that administrators don't have to start from scratch. There are practical, accessible tools that can be used to gather and present information in ways that are clear and empowering.

1. Surveys and Feedback Forms

Use post-event surveys, quarterly check-ins, or anonymous suggestion forms to capture honest input from attendees, volunteers, or team leaders. Tools like Google Forms, SurveyMonkey, or Typeform are user-friendly and free for basic use.

Make sure surveys:

- Are brief and specific
- Include a mix of quantitative ratings and open-ended questions
- Invite both praise and constructive suggestions

2. Dashboards and Data Visuals

Use spreadsheets, ChMS data, or dashboard tools to track attendance, giving, and engagement. Data doesn't have to be complex — a simple chart showing attendance growth over a few months can spark meaningful conversations.

Visual summaries help leadership teams:

- Spot trends
- Evaluate ministry health at a glance
- Make informed decisions

3. Annual Ministry Reports

Combine stories and statistics into an end-of-year report that reflects on the past 12 months. This not only celebrates impact but also encourages future engagement.

Include:

- Ministry highlights
- Financial summaries
- Volunteer acknowledgements
- Testimonies and photos

Make it something you can share with the congregation, not just the staff.

4. Team Reviews and Debriefs

After every major ministry initiative or event, hold a structured debrief session. Ask:

- What went well?
- What could we improve?
- What did God do that surprised or encouraged us?
- What would we change next time?

Encourage input from all levels of involvement, not just senior leaders.

Building a Culture of Review

Evaluation should not feel like a threat. When it becomes part of the normal rhythm of church life, people begin to view it as a tool for learning, growth, and celebration.

Administrators can help build this culture by:

Scheduling regular review sessions in the church calendar (e.g. end of term, post-event, quarterly reviews)

Setting a tone of encouragement – feedback is about growth, not blame

Celebrating wins publicly – use emails, team meetings, or Sunday moments to share what's going well

Sharing data in clear, accessible ways – don't overwhelm people with spreadsheets; summarise key insights simply

Inviting feedback across departments – evaluation should be multi-directional. Volunteers, staff, and congregants all have valuable perspectives

As evaluation becomes expected, teams become more open, reflective, and proactive in how they lead and serve.

Final Thoughts

You cannot improve what you don't evaluate. And you cannot evaluate well without clear systems, humble leadership, and a culture of trust. As an administrator, you are a steward of this process. You help ministry leaders move beyond gut feelings and assumptions into clarity, accountability, and celebration.

Measuring impact is not about numbers alone. It's about souls, service, and stewardship. It's about asking: Are we bearing fruit that lasts?

Are people growing in faith? Are our systems helping or hindering our mission?

When churches embrace evaluation, they grow — not just in size, but in depth. They become more focused, more united, and more fruitful.

So ask the questions. Gather the data. Share the stories. And always remember that faithful administration isn't just about keeping things running — it's about helping the Church run well.

Because in the Kingdom, fruit matters. And your leadership helps it grow.

The Administrator as a Bridge Builder

In any church, especially as it grows in size and scope, a natural challenge begins to emerge: ministries start to function in silos. Each department — worship, outreach, children's ministry, youth, discipleship, hospitality, and more — develops its own rhythm, priorities, and workflows. While each team may be working toward the same mission, without intentional alignment and communication, they often begin operating independently. The result can be confusion, duplication, and a slow erosion of unity.

This is where administrators play a vital, often unseen role — as bridge builders.

The administrator is uniquely positioned to work across all ministries. While not a department head, the administrator touches nearly every area of church life — from scheduling and budgeting to communication and coordination. This strategic vantage point provides a powerful opportunity to connect ministries, unify efforts, and help the Body of Christ function as one.

This chapter explores how administrators can fulfil the holy calling of bridge building: not just by managing logistics, but by knitting together hearts, teams, and vision.

Why Ministries Drift Apart

It's important to understand that ministry silos rarely form out of rebellion or disunity. More often, they arise accidentally, as teams grow and begin focusing deeply on their specific areas of responsibility. Over time, without regular check-ins or cross-departmental collaboration, even the most well-intentioned ministries can begin to drift apart.

This drift leads to several common issues:

Duplicated efforts – Two teams may plan separate events on the same weekend, unintentionally competing for volunteers, space, or congregational attention.

Resource strain – Multiple ministries may request the same equipment or budget allocations without realising it, creating conflict or inefficiency.

Communication breakdowns – Important announcements may get missed, and team leaders may feel out of the loop or unsupported.

Disunity in culture – When departments operate in isolation, the broader church vision becomes blurred. People start to speak different "languages," and the sense of being one church family weakens.

As administrators, we are not above these departments — but we often work across them. That unique position enables us to spot areas of overlap, misalignment, or tension and gently bring teams together for greater effectiveness and harmony.

Key Bridge-Building Functions

Building bridges isn't just philosophical — it's practical. There are tangible ways administrators can connect people, align plans, and cultivate unity across departments.

1. Calendar Coordination

One of the simplest but most impactful bridge-building tasks is maintaining a master calendar. This prevents scheduling clashes and ensures that major events do not compete for the same volunteers, space, or attention.

An administrator can:

> Facilitate quarterly calendar planning sessions with department heads
>
> Maintain a shared digital calendar (e.g. Google Calendar or Planning Centre)
>
> Flag potential conflicts and encourage collaboration between ministries

When the calendar is coordinated well, teams feel supported and empowered rather than crowded and confused.

2. Cross-Ministry Communication

Administrators can establish regular rhythms of communication between departments to help ensure shared understanding and cooperation.

This might include:

- Monthly or bi-monthly leadership meetings
- Shared updates via email or communication platforms
- A digital dashboard or bulletin board for key announcements and wins

Encouraging each team to share what they're doing, what they need, and how others can support them helps build relational trust and strategic alignment.

3. Resource Sharing

Budget constraints and space limitations can sometimes create tension. Administrators help by managing resources fairly and transparently, ensuring no one ministry feels overlooked or over-indulged.

This includes:

- Creating shared systems for booking rooms, tech equipment, or vehicles
- Managing budgets with fairness and clear communication
- Helping teams plan in advance so needs are anticipated and resourced appropriately

When ministries see that resources are allocated with wisdom and equity, they are more likely to collaborate and honour each other's needs.

4. Vision Alignment

The senior leadership team carries the overall vision of the church — but often, that vision must be translated into the day-to-day work of each department.

Administrators serve as vision interpreters, helping ministry teams:

- Understand how their goals connect to the bigger picture
- Clarify measurable objectives that align with church priorities
- Avoid "mission drift" by regularly revisiting the church's core values and goals

A bridge-building administrator doesn't just push tasks — they help teams see the why behind the what.

Relational Wisdom

Being a bridge builder isn't just about systems — it's also deeply relational. It requires emotional intelligence, spiritual maturity, and a heart for unity.

Some key postures for relational bridge-building include:

Listening without judgment – Ministry leaders may have frustrations, ideas, or insecurities. An administrator who listens well becomes a trusted confidant and advisor.

Clarifying without controlling – Instead of enforcing rules, the administrator seeks to bring clarity to roles, expectations, and plans — while honouring each ministry's unique voice.

Affirming value – Each department plays a vital role in the health of the church. Administrators should regularly affirm their contributions and speak life into their leaders.

Speaking multiple "languages" – Administrators must adapt their communication style when talking to tech teams, pastors, creatives, and intercessors. Flexibility and empathy are essential.

Bridge builders carry the tone of the organisation. When administrators lead with humility and grace, it sets the tone for collaboration and unity.

Cultivating a Culture of Togetherness

Beyond tasks, administrators help shape culture. When bridge building becomes part of the church's rhythm, ministries naturally begin to think more collectively. They start to ask:

How does this serve the whole church?

Who else needs to be involved in this conversation?

How can we collaborate rather than compete?

Administrators can foster this by:

- Encouraging cross-team prayer times
- Facilitating joint trainings or retreats
- Publicly celebrating when ministries work together successfully
- Modelling honour and appreciation in how they speak about all departments

Togetherness is not automatic — it must be cultivated. But when it becomes embedded in the culture, it multiplies health and fruitfulness across the board.

Final Thoughts

The Church doesn't thrive just because of what we do — but because of how we do it together. Disconnected ministries may still produce programmes, but unified ministries produce disciples. They reflect the oneness that Jesus prayed for — a Church that is not just busy, but beautifully coordinated.

Administrators who embrace their role as bridge builders serve the Body of Christ in powerful, often invisible ways. You are not just connecting calendars — you're connecting callings. You're not just aligning systems — you're aligning hearts.

This is more than administration — it's Kingdom architecture. And your careful, prayerful, Spirit-led bridge building creates a Church where every part is honoured, every team is equipped, and every ministry is moving forward as one body, under one Head, for one mission.

That's not just administration — that's a holy assignment.

The Calling and Commissioning of the Administrator

The gift of administration is one of the most under-celebrated, yet deeply vital, gifts in the Body of Christ. It is often mistaken for mere efficiency or organisation, tucked into the background of church life like stage hands behind a curtain. But make no mistake: administration is not simply a support role — it is a spiritual calling. A divine assignment. A ministry unto God.

In the Kingdom of God, every calling comes with a commissioning. Apostles are sent. Prophets are released. Evangelists are empowered. Shepherds are anointed. And so too, administrators are appointed — not by man's convenience, but by God's design. This final chapter is a declaration and a charge: to walk in your identity, serve with boldness, and build with eternal perspective.

Called by God, Not Just Needed by the Church

You were not chosen merely because there was a gap to fill. You were not the "available one," the "faithful helper," or the "only one who could get it done." You were called — intentionally, lovingly, strategically — by God. Before the need existed, the gift was planted in you.

Your attention to detail. Your ability to think ahead. Your gift for coordination, planning, and implementation. Your capacity to bring calm in chaos, order to confusion, and systems to vision. These are not personality quirks. They are evidence of divine craftsmanship.

You are not second-tier.

You are not less than.

You are not peripheral to the work of ministry.

You are set apart.

And just like the tabernacle builders in Exodus, or the ship's administrator in Acts 27, you have been chosen for a sacred task.

You are God's gift to the Church.

Commissioned to Lead

The gift of administration is not passive. It is a leadership gift. You may not always be the one holding the microphone, but you are often the one holding the structure that allows the microphone to be used well. You carry weight in the room — not because of title or visibility, but because of the authority and responsibility given to you by God.

As an administrator, you:

> Shape systems that sustain ministry – The behind-the-scenes flow that keeps services, events, and programmes running is often invisible — until it's missing. Your design is part of God's design.

Protect the peace and pace of leadership – You guard against burnout by creating sustainable rhythms. You hold the calendar, the budget, the communications — the tools that keep leaders focused on people, not just problems.

Build what others only imagine – Visionaries dream. You translate dreams into timelines, plans, and outcomes. You bring structure to strategy and accountability to ambition.

Connect vision to reality – You are the bridge between ideas and implementation, between inspiration and impact.

This is leadership. It may be quiet, but it is powerful. And it is needed now more than ever.

Your Spiritual Authority

As you walk in your gift, remember this: your strength is not in your systems. Your authority is not in your spreadsheets. It flows from your intimacy with God.

The most effective administrators are not just organised — they are spiritually attuned. They make prayer-soaked decisions. They ask God for insight before they ask the team for input. They are led by the Spirit, not just the calendar.

Let your authority flow from:

Daily surrender – Start with devotion, not just deadlines. Let your service be an overflow of worship.

Prayer-soaked decisions – Seek God's wisdom in every plan, every email, every conflict resolution.

Grace-filled communication – Use your words to build bridges, not barriers. Speak truth in love, and lead with both humility and clarity.

Unshakable trust in the God of order – Remember, the God who separated light from darkness is the God who guides your planning. He is not the author of confusion — He is the source of clarity.

You are more than an operational expert. You are a spiritual leader. An intercessor. An atmosphere-setter. A guardian of purpose.

A Charge to the Church

To every pastor, department head, and ministry leader: honour your administrators. Recognise the gift they carry. See beyond their task lists and deadlines. Involve them in the vision, not just in the execution.

Administrators need to be included in strategic conversations, resourced for their responsibilities, and covered in prayer just like any other ministry leader. When administrators are empowered, the entire church functions with greater clarity, effectiveness, and unity.

Don't wait until something goes wrong to appreciate them. Speak honour while the work is still being done. Call out the spiritual nature of their work. Equip them, encourage them, and thank them publicly and privately.

The Church is stronger when we function as one body — with every part recognised, empowered, and released into its purpose.

Final Thoughts: A Commissioning

To every administrator reading this, this is your commissioning:

Walk in your gift without apology.

You are not "just" an organiser or scheduler. You are anointed for this. You carry divine insight for divine impact.

Lead with wisdom, courage, and grace.

You don't need to be loud to be bold. Lead with quiet strength, with steady faith, and with servant-hearted excellence.

Build with eternity in mind.

Every meeting you schedule, every system you create, every plan you finalise is not just administrative — it's eternal. It's preparing the ground for lives to be changed, for people to be discipled, for the Kingdom to be revealed.

And know this: heaven sees what you build in secret.

When no one else notices the early setup or the late-night planning, heaven sees. When you hold others up, create order out of chaos, or stay faithful behind the scenes — heaven sees.

You are not behind the scenes.

You are at the foundation.

And the Church needs you more than ever.

So go. Lead. Build.

Let the gift of administration rise in full maturity.

Let your systems reflect the Spirit's wisdom.

Let your leadership release others into theirs.

Let your presence cultivate peace, purpose, and unity.

You are not a convenience — you are a calling.

And the Kingdom of God needs you.

Printed in Dunstable, United Kingdom

64756133R00129